REINVENT YOUR THINKING; TRANSFORM YOUR LIFE

A Blueprint to Unlock Your Full Potential for Success and Achievement

Emmanuel Jones

DEDICATION

This book is dedicated to my parents, Chief Isaac Jones-Udokpan and Mrs Cecilia Jones-Udokpan, who from the beginning of my life, prepared me for the future.

To those who are still in the valley and quagmire of indecision, and yet to find their purpose in life.

To those who are stuck in their journey of destiny, and are still searching for the silver lining of the cloud of their struggles, challenges and difficulties.

May this book equip you with the tools to reinvent, redefine, upgrade and unstick yourself to create the future you desire.

I wrote this book from the lessons I learned from my reinvention journey. May this book be your tour guide to take you from the pit of life to your promised land, and to deliver my desire for you that the rest of your life will be the best of your life.

CONTENTS

Acknowledgements

I wish to express my appreciation to the exceptional people who have contributed in many ways to make this book a reality.

First and foremost, I thank the Almighty God for His great grace and marvellous mercies granted me in my reinvention journey to finally birth this dream after several masterclass seminars on this topic. To Him alone be the glory.

I sincerely celebrate my wife, Pastor Alvinah, from whom I have learned so much about the importance of love and family. She shares her thinking with me daily, and I appreciate her unusual encouragement and uncommon support. She practically runs my life to provoke positive thinking. Alvinah, you are my mainstay and my greatest inspiration. You are remarkable, you are phenomenal.

I also appreciate my Dream Team:

Idara Jones, my personal writer and editor. Her enthusiasm for writing and her wisdom are phenomenal.

Ini Jones, my media consultant. She helps me with social media, and facilitates my Masterclass seminars behind the scenes.

And Emem Jones, who motivates and encourages me.

My special thanks to Dr. N. Nwokolo for her encouragement, and for editing and proofreading the original manuscript. Thank you for your time.

I appreciate all the staff and the leadership team at Jones Foundation, for the years we have worked together with a vision of helping others to succeed, in our many Masterclass, Mastermind, Business and Leadership seminars and conferences.

I am very grateful to Madame Merola, the B.A.N.G creator, my image and personal branding consultant. She added the finishing touches and carried out the final proofreading and editing of this book.

Finally, to all members of the Redeemed Christian Church of God, Fountain of Grace, Wolverhampton, UK, I appreciate and thank you for your labour and sacrifice of love, and for allowing me to set aside the time for writing this book.   You   are   a   wonderful   family!

FORWARD

In the journey of life, we are all explorers, seeking to uncover the mysteries of our existence, striving to navigate the complexities of our world, and yearning for transformation. "Reinvent Your Thinking, Transform Your Life" is a beacon of enlightenment that guides us along this profound expedition.

In the pages that follow, you will embark on a transformative odyssey, one that challenges your perspectives, redefines your beliefs, and empowers you to forge a path to a better you.
The power of thought, the cornerstone of our individual and collective destinies, is dissected and illuminated.
Through the wisdom shared in these words, you will come to understand that within the realm of your thoughts lies the key to the life you desire.

The author, with meticulous care and deep insight, navigates the intricacies of human cognition, leading us through the labyrinth of our minds. It's a journey filled with revelations, offering a profound realization: we have the power to reshape our thinking and, in doing so, to transform our lives.

"Reinvent Your Thinking, Transform Your Life" is not a mere collection of ideas but a blueprint for self-discovery and renewal.
It presents a series of practical tools, strategies, and anecdotes that empower you to challenge the status quo and reimagine your possibilities. It's an invitation to break free from the confines of limiting beliefs, to

embrace change, and to embark on a journey toward personal and spiritual growth.

This book isn't just a collection of words; it's a roadmap for those seeking to break free from limitations, embrace change, and unlock the power of a renewed mindset.
The Author's insights resonate with the profound and timeless wisdom written in the scripture recorded in Proverbs 23:7a which says,
"For as he thinks in his heart, so is he."

As you delve into these pages, be prepared to embark on a profound expedition—a voyage that transcends the boundaries of self-doubt, fear, and uncertainty. Allow yourself to be guided by the author's wisdom, and, in doing so, discover the incredible potential that resides within you.

"Reinvent Your Thinking, Transform Your Life" is a testament to the limitless capacity of the human spirit for growth and evolution. May this book inspire you, equip you, and empower you to embark on your own journey of transformation. May it be the catalyst for a more profound understanding of yourself and your world.

I commend the author for offering us this valuable compass to navigate the often tumultuous seas of life. As you read, absorb, and apply the principles within, I am confident that you will find your life enriched and your thinking forever transformed.

With great anticipation for the journey that lies ahead.

Pastor Leke Sanusi
Continental Overseer, RCCG, Europe.
Chairman, Board of Trustee, Redeemed Christian Church of God(RCCG), United Kingdom

Introduction

Introducing "Reinvent Your Thinking, Transform Your Life" - an empowering new book that delves into the incredible power of our thoughts and the profound impact they have on our lives. In this transformative guide, we explore how our mindset shapes our reality, and how we can harness its potential to create a life of fulfilment, success, and happiness.

Drawing upon a wealth of research, personal anecdotes, and practical strategies, this book offers a roadmap to help you break free from limiting beliefs, overcome self-doubt, and unlock your true potential. Whether you are seeking personal growth, career advancement, or improved relationships, "Reinvent Your Thinking, Transform Your Life" provides the tools and insights needed to embark on a remarkable journey of self-discovery and transformation.

Through the pages of this book, you will discover how to cultivate a positive and resilient mindset, reframe challenges as opportunities, and develop effective strategies to overcome obstacles. You will learn how to tap into your inner strength, embrace change, and create a life that aligns with your deepest desires and values.

"Reinvent Your Thinking, Transform Your Life" will inspire and empower you to take charge of your thoughts, rewrite your story, and live a life that is authentically yours.

Get ready to embark on a transformative journey that will revolutionise the way you think, feel, and experience life.

I have you in mind as I write this book; it serves as a blueprint to unlock your full potential for success and achievement.

See you at the TOP!

Emmanuel Jones

CHAPTER 1

Unlocking the Unspoken:
A Journey from Stuttering to Self-Discovery

'For as he thinks in his heart, so is he.'
-Proverbs 23:7a

In the quiet, remote village of Ikot Ekot, Etinan, Akwa Ibom State, Nigeria, where I was born, traditions and customs governed daily life. But it was not just the age-old customs that shaped my childhood; it was an inherent challenge I carried from birth.

You see, my parents, by an unexpected twist of fate, were both stammerers, and this was a hereditary gift they unwittingly passed down to me. Growing up in this picturesque, yet speech-centric village, my stammer became not just a quirk, but a formidable barrier, an ever-present obstacle to navigate through life.

Childhood, for many, is a time of carefree laughter and playful interactions. Yet for me it was a different narrative. The words I wished to speak seemed forever locked within, concealed by the constant struggle to articulate even the simplest of thoughts. My friends called me 'Stammer,' and the playground became a battleground where I fought not only to play, but to fit in.

As I entered the classroom, another ordeal awaited. While my classmates answered questions with ease, I laboured for hours just to utter a single word, much to the amusement of my peers. The weight of my stuttering words burdened my youthful shoulders, shrouding me in frustration and self-doubt. My quest was not just to find my voice, but to shatter the chains that held it captive.

Yet, in the heart of our village, on market days a different world came to life. The bustling marketplace was a place of vibrant interactions, where negotiations were not conducted in quiet aisles, but through the dance of words. It was a place where you had to speak your needs and defend your family's purse, a place that demanded clear and confident communication. Here, another layer of the challenge emerged, one that pushed me to confront my speech impediment head-on.

But as life often does, it presented me with a twist of fate. My parents' stammers became my inheritance, and my voice found itself ensnared in a web of silent struggles. While others bartered and bantered effortlessly, I grappled for words that eluded me. My stutter was not confined to the marketplace; it cast its shadow over my classroom, dimming my ability to participate and be heard.

Yet as the pages of my life turned, so did the narrative. One seemingly ordinary day held a profound moment. As I sought solace in the words of the Bible, a verse leapt out at me like a beacon of hope:

'For as he thinks in his heart, so is he' (Proverbs 23:7a).

This simple statement unleashed a powerful revelation within me, igniting a new perspective on my circumstances. In that singular moment, a transformation began. I started to explore the uncharted territory concealed within my own mind, seeking to reshape my stuttering speech into a more promising future.

As I meditated and thought about that Bible verse, it changed my paradigm. It altered the way I saw myself, my attitude changed, and the stuttering that had hindered my future began to give way. My new thinking transformed my life and gave me a new experience.

With unwavering determination and a fresh perspective, I embarked on a journey of self-discovery and personal reinvention. Perseverance overcomes difficulties. With each day, as I persevered in meditating on my new perspective, my life began to turn around. I started speaking. I was empowered from within. My words began to flow more freely, my self-assurance grew, and the trajectory of my life underwent a profound transformation.

This is what this book is all about. It does not matter what your situation is; if you can reinvent your thinking, it will transform your life and give you a new experience.

My life's story has been a journey from silence to self-discovery, a journey that proves the power of the human spirit to transcend its limitations and redefine its destiny.

Welcome to a transformative journey that will unlock the immense power within your mind, guiding you towards a life filled with purpose, fulfilment and boundless opportunities.

This book, "Reinvent Your Thinking, Transform Your Life," serves as a guide that transcends the boundaries of conventional thought. It extends an invitation to you to explore the untapped potential of your mind and embrace the possibilities of an extraordinary existence.

Inventor Thomas Edison once said: *"Five percent of the people think; ten percent of the people think they think; and the other eighty-five percent would rather die than think."*

Recognizing the immense value of proper thinking, it is safe to say that we should aspire to be among the five percent!

Drawing on contemporary research in psychology, neuroscience and personal development, this book offers a comprehensive toolkit to help you harness the power of your thoughts and tap into your innate potential.

In the journey of life, one's mind is the compass that guides one through the twists and turns, challenges and triumphs. It is within the confines of our thoughts that our dreams are born and aspirations take shape. Our thoughts are the architects of our reality, holding the key to unlocking a life of fulfilment and success.

The human mind is an astonishing instrument, capable of shaping reality, overcoming obstacles and effecting profound changes in our lives. However, many of us find ourselves constrained by limiting beliefs, negative thought patterns and self-doubt. These constraints may be holding us back from the true potential that lies within us, depriving us of the joy and accomplishments we deserve.

Within these pages, you will embark on a voyage of self-discovery, learning how to break free from the shackles of old, unproductive habits and thought processes. The key to unlocking this potential lies in our ability to reinvent our thinking - to embrace a mindset that empowers, uplifts and propels us towards the life that we have always envisioned.

Throughout this journey, you will encounter a treasure trove of transformative techniques, practices and insights that will empower you to:

- *Identify and challenge self-limiting beliefs:*
  We will uncover the beliefs that have held you back and replace them with empowering, growth-oriented ones, igniting a new sense of confidence and self-belief.

- *Embrace resilience and change:*

Life is an ever-changing journey, and learning to adapt and thrive amidst uncertainty is crucial. Discover how to cultivate resilience, and open your mind to embrace new possibilities fearlessly.

- *Cultivate a positive mindset:*
  By shifting your focus to gratitude and positivity, you will awaken an innate sense of appreciation for life's blessings, and forge a path towards greater contentment and joy.

- *Master the art of visualisation:*
  We will delve into the profound technique of creative visualisation, enabling you to turn your dreams into reality and propel yourself towards your goals.

- *Take inspired action:*
  Equipped with renewed purpose and vision, you will learn to take inspired and intentional actions towards the life you desire, becoming the architect of your destiny.

- *Cultivate a growth mindset:*
  You will embrace the transformative power of continuous learning, seeing challenges as opportunities for growth and using setbacks as stepping stones towards success.

- *Establish a harmonious and purposeful life:*
  As you shed old thought patterns and embrace new ways of thinking, you will witness the emergence of a life aligned with your true purpose, passions and values.

By the time you reach the final pages of this book, you will be equipped with the tools to rewrite the script of your life. You will emerge with a heightened sense of self-awareness and a profound appreciation for the power that resides within your mind. As you reinvent your thinking, you will open the doors to a life of abundance, phenomenal achievement, success and fulfilment.

The journey ahead will not be without its challenges, but with every step you take, you will draw closer to the extraordinary life that awaits you.

The power is in your hands, and the time to embrace change is now. Let us embark on this transformative journey together, eager to embrace the infinite possibilities that lie within you, ready to transform your life, create a life that transcends the boundaries of imagination, and shape your destiny.

Welcome to the beginning of your extraordinary story.

Reinvention Tip 1:

Reflective Exercises: Unveiling Your Unspoken Moments

Take a moment to delve into the depths of your own experiences and uncover the moments when your voice felt confined or your thoughts struggled to find expression. Reflect on instances in your life where you may have felt unheard or held back from fully sharing your authentic self.

Guiding Questions:

1. Recall a specific moment when you hesitated to speak up. What were the circumstances, and what held you back?

2. Think about a time when you felt your thoughts or ideas were not given the attention they deserved. How did it make you feel, and what impact did it have on your self-perception?

3. Consider situations where societal expectations or norms constrained your ability to express yourself freely. What were those expectations, and how did they influence your communication?
4. Reflect on instances where you felt a disconnection between your inner thoughts and your outward expression. What emotions accompanied this dissonance?

Journaling Prompts:

1.Describe the emotions you associate with these unspoken moments. Were there feelings of frustration, self-doubt, or a longing to be understood?

2.In what ways have these experiences shaped your communication style and impacted your sense of self?
3. Imagine a scenario where you could express yourself without any barriers. What would that look like, and how would you feel?

This reflective exercise is an initial step on your journey of unlocking the unspoken. Take your time to ponder these questions and capture your thoughts in a journal or a dedicated space. As you explore these moments, you lay the foundation for a transformative voyage toward self-discovery and authentic expression.

CHAPTER 2

Everything Begins with a Thought

"Our thoughts are the architects of our destiny."
- David O. McKay

"Watch your thoughts, they become words; watch your words, they become actions; watch your actions, they become habits; watch your habits, they become character; watch your character, for it becomes your destiny."
- Lao Tzu

Having donned my graduation cap and walked across that stage, I was filled with hope and excitement about the adventures life had in store for me. I had just earned my qualification as a Radiographer, and the possibilities seemed boundless. Little did I know that the ominous shadow of unemployment would soon loom over my dreams.

In my homeland, Nigeria, the path for fresh graduates was via compulsory service in the National Youth Service Corps (NYSC). A year of voluntary paramilitary service awaited me, a stepping stone to my professional journey. The reality of this endeavour was harsher than I had imagined.

My NYSC posting landed me in a private X-ray centre in Calabar, Cross River State. It should have been a platform for me to grow, learn and thrive, but my employer had other ideas. For an entire year, I toiled diligently, devoting my skills and dedication to the work. In return, he paid me a pittance, a wage that did not in any way reflect the value of my contributions. And as the year's end approached, he made a choice I found both disheartening and unjust - he chose not to retain my services.

Leaving that place, I felt a mixture of dejection and uncertainty. The world seemed to be closing in on me, and I could not help but think that my ambitions were slipping away. But deep within, there was a flicker of hope, a tiny voice that whispered, *"This is just the beginning."*

I embarked on a new journey, this time seeking opportunities in a teaching hospital. Hope had not abandoned me entirely, and I clung to the belief that my skills would eventually find a home. My path led me to the Ahmadu Bello University Teaching Hospital in Zaria, Kaduna. An interview awaited, and I entered it with the anticipation of a fresh start.

I performed well at the interview, but despite my qualifications and dedication, tribalism reared its ugly head. I was denied the position solely due to origins I could not control, and the weight of rejection was crushing.

In that dark moment, it was easy to believe that my dreams had been shattered and that I would forever be held back by circumstances beyond my control.

But I had learned a powerful truth - *everything begins with a thought.* I had the power to transform my thinking, and in doing so to transform my life. It was not the end; it was the beginning of something extraordinary.

Soon, an invitation arrived, one that would change the course of my life. A second interview, this time at the Obafemi Awolowo University Teaching Hospital in Ile Ife, Oyo State, Nigeria. I journeyed there, fuelled by the belief that what I had to offer should extend beyond tribal boundaries.

The interview was a turning point, a chance for me to prove my mettle and demonstrate my capabilities. The winds of change were in the air, and my new way of thinking was my guiding star.

After the interview, the words I had been longing to hear were finally spoken. I was offered the position I had worked so hard for, a testament to the power of self-belief and resilience. My journey, marked by adversity and challenges, had been a journey of transformation. It clearly illustrated the profound impact of thought, and the truth of the statement, *"Everything begins with a thought."*

This chapter is not just the story of my journey; it demonstrates the principle that with the right mindset and unwavering determination, we can rewrite our destinies, no matter the obstacles in our path.

It was just the beginning, and the journey ahead held the promise of a brighter, more fulfilling future.

"Everything begins with a thought."
These simple yet profound words hold the essence of human existence and the very fabric of reality. In this chapter, we delve into the power of thoughts, exploring how they shape our lives and influence the world around us.

The Birth of an Idea:
Ideas, inventions, and masterpieces all originate from a single seed called a thought.

Throughout history, great philosophers, scientists, artists, and innovators have acknowledged the transformative power of their initial musings. From the ancient philosophers of Greece to modern-day entrepreneurs, the power of thought has been a constant driving force for progress.

The Anatomy of Thought:
In this chapter, I will dissect the intricate components that constitute the anatomy of thought. We will explore together how thoughts can be nurtured, reshaped, and guided to create a harmonious symphony of ideas and actions. Just as a surgeon studies the human body to heal and enhance it, we will study the anatomy of thought to cultivate a more profound connection with our inner selves.

As we dive into the complexities of thought, we will uncover the threads that connect us to our desires, our aspirations, and the world around us. Let us unravel the secrets of the anatomy of thought, for within its depths lies the power to sculpt the life we envision.

Thoughts are more than mere fleeting moments in our minds; they are intricate processes that connect our conscious and subconscious realms. The brain, a complex network of neurons and synapses, orchestrates these thoughts. As we learn to understand the mechanics of thoughts, we unlock the potential to shape them purposefully.

Within the intricate labyrinth of the mind, thoughts emerge as the pulsating heartbeats of our consciousness. Like intricate machinery, thoughts possess their own anatomy - a system of interconnected components that contribute to the symphony of our inner world. Understanding this anatomy is the key to harnessing the full potential of our cognitive faculties.

At the core of the anatomy of thought lies perception. Our senses act as the gateways, allowing external stimuli to infiltrate our consciousness. Every sensation, every sight, sound, taste, touch, and scent, is a catalyst for thought. Our experiences are the building blocks of cognition, shaping the lens through which we perceive reality.

From perception springs emotion, an integral part of the thought process. Emotions infuse our thoughts with colour and intensity, colouring them with shades of joy, sorrow, anger, or tranquillity. These emotions form the bridge between the physical world and our mental landscapes, influencing the directions our thoughts take.

Once emotions take root, cognition commences. Our thoughts begin to formulate, weaving connections between memories, beliefs, and desires. This intricate dance of neural pathways creates the tapestry of thought. Just as a skilled composer orchestrates music, we orchestrate our thoughts by choosing the elements to include and the patterns to weave.

However, the anatomy of thought doesn't end here. Action is the culmination of thought - the manifestation of our inner world into the external reality. The decisions we make, the goals we set, and the steps we take are all reflections of our thoughts brought to life. Just as a sculptor moulds clay into form, we mould our aspirations and intentions into tangible achievements.

Understanding the anatomy of thought empowers us to be deliberate architects of our mental landscapes. By recognizing the role of perception, emotion, cognition, and action, we gain the ability to shape our thoughts with intention. We become navigators, steering the ship of consciousness through the vast ocean of possibilities.

The Law of Attraction:
The Law of Attraction states that like attracts like, meaning positive thoughts attract positive outcomes, and negative thoughts draw negative experiences. By understanding this principle, we can harness the power of our thoughts to manifest our desires and create the reality we envision.

The Law of Attraction is a powerful concept that suggests that your thoughts, emotions and beliefs play a significant role in shaping your reality. It posits that by focusing on positive thoughts and emotions, you can attract positive outcomes and experiences into your life, while negative thoughts and emotions can bring about undesirable results.

Key principles of the Law of Attraction include:

1. Like Attracts Like
This fundamental principle suggests that the energy you emit, whether positive or negative, will attract similar energy and experiences. If you constantly think about lack and negativity, you are likely to attract more of the same into your life. Conversely, a positive and abundant mindset can draw positive circumstances.

2. The Power of Thoughts
Thoughts are seen as powerful tools for shaping your reality. By consistently focusing on your desires and believing in the possibility of their attainment, you increase the likelihood of manifesting them.

3. Emotions Matter
Emotions are considered the fuel for the Law of Attraction. The stronger the positive emotions associated with your desires, the more likely they are to manifest. Feeling gratitude, joy and belief can accelerate the attraction process.

4. Clarity and Specificity
Clearly defining your desires and goals is crucial. Vague or contradictory thoughts can hinder the manifestation process. The more specific and detailed your intentions, the easier it is for God to respond.

5. Belief and Faith

Belief in the process of the Law of Attraction is essential. Doubt and scepticism can block its effectiveness. Cultivating faith and trust in God's ability to deliver your desires is vital.

6. Taking Inspired Action

While the Law of Attraction emphasises the power of thoughts and emotions, it is not about wishful thinking alone. Taking inspired action towards your goals is an important part of the process. God may guide you toward opportunities, but you must be willing to act on them.

7. Gratitude and Positivity

Expressing gratitude for what you already have can amplify the positive energy you emit. It shifts your focus from lack to abundance, and attracts more of the things you appreciate.

8. Patience and Timing

Manifestation does not always happen instantly. It may take time for your desires to materialise. Trust in divine timing, and remain patient throughout the process.

9. Letting Go

Paradoxically, the Law of Attraction also involves letting go of the desperate need for your desires to manifest. A sense of detachment and trust that your intentions will come to fruition can be crucial.

10. Awareness and Self-Reflection

Self-awareness is key to recognizing and reshaping your thought patterns. Regular self-reflection allows you to identify and change any negative beliefs or emotions that may be blocking your desires.

The Law of Attraction is a versatile concept that can be applied to various aspects of life, from personal development to relationships and career success. While it has gained popularity, it is important to approach it with a balanced perspective, combining belief in its potential with practical action and self-awareness.

From Thought to Action
Thoughts alone cannot bring about change; they require action to manifest into tangible results. This step often presents the greatest challenge, as fear, doubt, and uncertainty can paralyse us. Discovering how to bridge the gap between thought and action empowers us to materialise our dreams and ambitions.

The Impact on Mental Health
Our thoughts play a significant role in our mental well-being. Negative thought patterns can lead to stress, anxiety, and depression, while positive and constructive thoughts promote emotional resilience and happiness. We explore strategies to identify and modify detrimental thought patterns to foster a healthier mental landscape.

From Individual to Collective Thoughts
Thoughts not only shape the lives of individuals, but also impact the collective consciousness of societies and civilizations. Cultural paradigms, social norms, and political ideologies are all products of the collective thoughts of a group. Understanding this collective power can guide us in steering societies towards progress and harmony.

The Ripple Effect
The power of thoughts extends beyond the individual and collective realms, creating a ripple effect that transcends borders and time. The thoughts of one person can inspire countless others, igniting movements, sparking revolutions, and changing the course of history. By recognizing the potential impact of our thoughts, we become conscious creators of a better world.

The Ripple Effect refers to the idea that a single action or event can have far-reaching consequences, creating a series of impacts that spread outward like ripples in water. It is often used to describe how small actions can lead to larger changes or influence various aspects of a situation or system.

The Dance of Thoughts and Emotions

Thoughts and emotions are intricately intertwined, influencing each other in a continuous dance. Understanding this dynamic interplay allows us to cultivate emotional intelligence, empowering us to channel our emotions to serve our highest aspirations.

Thoughts and the Quest for Wisdom

Throughout human history, sages, mystics, and seekers of truth have explored the depths of consciousness, seeking wisdom beyond the realms of ordinary thought. By delving into the realms of meditation, mindfulness, and introspection, we unlock a deeper connection to our thoughts and their source, transcending the limitations of our minds.

In this chapter, we have embarked on a journey to uncover the significance of thoughts in shaping our lives and the world we live. The understanding that everything begins with a thought empowers us to take charge of our minds, embrace our creative potential, and co-create a reality aligned with our highest aspirations. By harnessing the power of our thoughts, we become architects of our destiny and participants in the ever-evolving tapestry of existence.

REINVENTION TIP 2:

1. What thoughts come to mind when you hear the phrase "everything begins with a thought"? How does this concept resonate with you personally?

2. Take a moment to reflect on a recent accomplishment or success in your life. Can you trace it back to the initial thought or idea that sparked it? How does this realization impact your perspective on the power of thoughts?

3. Consider a current challenge or obstacle you're facing. How might shifting your thoughts or mindset around this situation influence your ability to overcome it? Brainstorm a few alternative thoughts or perspectives that could empower you in dealing with the challenge.

4. Reflect on a time when a negative thought or limiting belief held you back from pursuing a goal or taking action. How did that thought impact your actions and outcomes? What lessons can you learn from this experience to better harness the power of positive thinking in the future?

5. Imagine a future goal or aspiration that you have. Spend a few moments visualizing and mentally exploring the thoughts and beliefs that would support your success. How can you cultivate and nurture these empowering thoughts to propel you towards your desired outcome?

Remember to take your time with these reflection exercises and write down your thoughts and insights. Use this opportunity to gain deeper self-awareness and uncover ways to harness the power of thoughts in your life.

CHAPTER 3

Winning the Battles of Your Mind

"To win the battle of the mind, you must become the master of your thoughts, not their servant."
- Brian Tracy

I read a story of a young man called Arjun. He was known for his intelligence and creativity, but he struggled with self-doubt and negative thoughts that often held him back from realising his true potential.

Arjun had a deep passion for painting, and he dreamed of becoming a renowned artist. However, every time he picked up a paintbrush, his mind would fill with thoughts like, "You're not good enough," or "No one will appreciate your art." These thoughts became a constant barrier, preventing him from expressing his creativity freely.

One day, a wise old man named Guruji came to the village. Guruji was known for his profound wisdom and the ability to guide people through their inner struggles.
Arjun decided to seek Guruji's guidance, and went to him with a heavy heart.

Guruji listened patiently to Arjun's story, and then said, "My dear boy, the battle you are fighting is not with your paintbrush or canvas, but within your own mind. To become a great artist, you must first win the battle of the mind."

Guruji proposed a challenge to Arjun. He told him to spend the next month painting a single canvas without any self-criticism, doubt, or negative thoughts. Arjun was puzzled, but accepted the challenge, eager to overcome his mental barriers.

As Arjun painted, his mind began to race with doubts and fears, just as before. However, each time a negative thought arose, he remembered Guruji's words and pushed them aside. He focused solely on the strokes of his brush, the interplay of colours, and the emotions he wanted to convey through his art.

Days turned into weeks, and Arjun's painting began to transform. It was filled with vibrant colours, intricate details, and a sense of passion that he had never felt before. He was so engrossed in his work that he lost track of time and his worries.

Finally, the day of reckoning arrived. Arjun presented his completed painting to Guruji. Guruji examined it with a smile and said, "You have won the battle of the mind, Arjun. Your painting is not just a masterpiece on canvas; it is a symbol of your victory over self-doubt and negativity."

Arjun realised that he had indeed conquered his inner demons. He felt a newfound sense of confidence and freedom. He continued to paint with passion and determination, and his art began to gain recognition far and wide.

Arjun's story spread throughout the village, inspiring others to confront their own battles of the mind. He became not only a successful artist, but also a mentor, helping people overcome their fears and embrace their true potential.

And so Arjun's journey of winning the battle of the mind became a legend, reminding everyone that true victory is not just in external accomplishments, but in the triumph over one's own inner struggles.

Defining Mental Battles:
Navigating the Landscape of the Mind

Mental battles are the intricate and often tumultuous conflicts that unfold within the intricate corridors of our minds. These battles manifest as the struggles, challenges, and confrontations we face on the psychological plane, influencing our thoughts, emotions, and overall mental well-being.

At the core of mental battles lies the interplay of opposing forces – positive versus negative thoughts, empowering beliefs versus limiting self-perceptions, and resilience versus vulnerability. These battles are deeply personal, as they are shaped by our unique experiences, fears, aspirations, and the complex tapestry of our individual psyches.

These conflicts can take various forms, ranging from self-doubt and inner criticism to grappling with anxiety, stress, and the weight of societal expectations. They emerge when our thoughts clash with our desires, when limiting beliefs challenge our potential, and when emotional triggers provoke intense internal struggles.

In essence, mental battles are the arenas where we confront the complexities of our own minds. They can arise from external influences or internal dialogues, propelling us into a dynamic interplay of thoughts and emotions. Acknowledging and understanding these battles is the first step in navigating the intricate landscape of the mind.

Confronting mental battles is not about eradicating challenges but about developing the resilience and awareness needed to navigate them effectively. It involves cultivating a deep understanding of our thought patterns, recognizing emotional triggers, and fostering the ability to choose empowering perspectives over self-limiting beliefs.

In this exploration, we embark on a journey to define, understand, and ultimately triumph over mental battles. It is a journey of self-discovery, resilience-building, and the realization that within the complexities of our minds, we hold the power to transform challenges into opportunities for growth.

Winning and Mastering the Battlefield of the Mind:

In the epic journey of life, the battleground of the mind stands as the arena where victories are forged and destinies are shaped. To win the battle of the mind is to conquer the very essence of one's existence, transcending challenges and unlocking the door to personal triumph. In this chapter, we explore strategies and insights to navigate this profound battlefield and emerge victorious in the war waged within.

Steps to Winning the Battle of the Mind:

1. Develop Awareness and Mindfulness:
The first step in winning the battle of the mind is to develop awareness of your thoughts and emotions. Take

time to observe your inner dialogue and identify any negative or self-limiting beliefs. Practice mindfulness to stay present in the moment and prevent your mind from wandering into unproductive or negative thought patterns.

2. Understanding the Terrain:
Before engaging in any battle, a wise strategist studies the terrain. Similarly, understanding the landscape of your mind is crucial. Reflect on your thoughts, beliefs, and emotions. Identify patterns that either propel you forward or hold you back. Awareness is the first step towards gaining mastery over the battlefield.

3. The Power of Perspective:
In the theatre of the mind, perspective reigns supreme. Challenge negative thoughts and reframe them into opportunities for growth. Recognize that your perspective shapes your reality. Choose to view challenges as stepping stones rather than stumbling blocks, and you'll already be changing the course of the battle.

4. Challenge Negative Thoughts:
Negative thoughts can be detrimental to our mental well-being and hinder our progress. Learn to challenge and reframe negative thoughts by questioning their validity and replacing them with positive and empowering affirmations. Develop a habit of focusing on the positive aspects of situations and finding opportunities for growth and learning.

5. Guarding the Gates:

The mind is susceptible to external influences that can sway its direction. Guard the gates of your mind diligently. Be mindful of the information you consume, the people you surround yourself with, and the environments you expose yourself to. Protecting your mental space is key to maintaining a resilient and focused mindset.

6. Arming Yourself with Positivity:
Positive affirmations and thoughts are your most potent weapons. Arm yourself with positivity daily. Cultivate a mindset that seeks solutions, embraces challenges, and finds opportunities in adversity. Your thoughts, like a well-forged sword, can cut through the toughest of circumstances.

7. Strategic Retreats - The Power of Silence:
In the midst of the battle, there is immense power in silence. Practice mindfulness and meditation to retreat to a mental sanctuary. In silence, you can observe your thoughts without being consumed by them. This strategic retreat allows you to recharge, gain clarity, and return to the battle with renewed vigor.

8. Mastering Emotional Intelligence:
Understanding and managing emotions is a crucial aspect of winning the battle of the mind. Emotional intelligence empowers you to navigate the stormy seas of feelings, ensuring they become tools for growth rather than destructive forces. Learn to respond, not react, to the ebb and flow of emotions.

9. Visualize Success:

Utilize the power of visualization to create a mental image of your desired outcome. Imagine yourself achieving your goals, experiencing success, and overcoming obstacles. Visualize the steps you need to take to reach your goals and imagine yourself taking those steps with confidence and determination. Regularly visualize your success to reinforce a positive mindset and motivate yourself to take action.

Envision your victories before they manifest in reality. Visualization is a potent tool for shaping your destiny. Create mental images of success, rehearse positive outcomes, and let your mind familiarize itself with the taste of triumph. The more vividly you can visualize success, the closer you are to achieving it.

10. Continuous Reinforcement:
Winning the battle of the mind is not a one-time triumph; it's a continuous process. Reinforce positive habits and thought patterns consistently. Regularly revisit your mental strategies, adjust them as needed, and celebrate the small victories along the way. The cumulative effect of these efforts is a resilient and victorious mind.

In conclusion, the battle of the mind is both an art and a science. It demands self-awareness, discipline, and a commitment to continuous improvement. By understanding the terrain, embracing positivity, and mastering the art of mental resilience, you can emerge triumphant in this epic battle, shaping a destiny that reflects the true power of your mind.

Understanding the Mind-Body Connection
- Exploring the intricate relationship between thoughts, emotions, and physical well-being.
- The impact of positive thinking on overall health and happiness.

The Subconscious Mind
- Uncovering the hidden influences of the subconscious on decision-making and behaviour.
- Techniques to reprogramme limiting beliefs and foster a growth mindset.
- Recognizing negative thought patterns

Identifying Cognitive Distortions
- Common cognitive distortions that cloud judgement and hinder personal development.
- Learning to challenge and replace distorted thoughts with constructive ones.

The Impact of Self-Talk
- Analysing the effects of self-talk on self-esteem and confidence.
- Practising self-compassion and cultivating a supportive inner dialogue.
- Strategies for Winning the Battle

Mindfulness and Meditation
- The practice of mindfulness to increase awareness of thoughts and emotions.
- Benefits of meditation in reducing stress and enhancing mental clarity.

Cognitive Behavioural Therapy (CBT)
- Utilising CBT techniques to restructure negative thought patterns.
- Transforming unhealthy behaviours and fostering resilience.

Visualisation and Affirmations
- The power of visualisation in achieving personal goals and success.
- Crafting positive affirmations to reinforce a growth-oriented mindset.
- Nurturing a positive mindset

Gratitude and Appreciation
- Embracing gratitude as a tool for fostering contentment and resilience.
- Practising appreciation for life's blessings and opportunities.

Embracing Failure and Growth
- Shifting the perspective on failure and viewing it as a stepping stone to growth.
- Embracing challenges and learning from setbacks.

The battle of the mind is a lifelong journey that requires commitment, self-awareness, and practice. By understanding the power of our thoughts and beliefs, recognizing negative thought patterns, and implementing effective strategies, we can foster a resilient and positive mindset to overcome life's challenges and achieve personal growth and success.

Remember, winning the battle of your mind is not a one-time victory, but a continuous effort that will transform your life for the better. Embrace the journey, and the rewards will be immeasurable.

REINVENTION TIP 3:

Embrace a growth mindset by viewing challenges as opportunities for learning and improvement. Shift your perspective from fixed beliefs to a more flexible and adaptive mindset, allowing yourself to overcome obstacles with resilience and continuous self-development.

Reflective Exercises:
1. Challenge Negative Thoughts:
   - Identify recurring negative thoughts.
   - Examine the evidence supporting and opposing these thoughts.
   - Develop more balanced and constructive perspectives.

2. Success Journal:
   - Keep a daily journal highlighting small wins and positive moments.

- Reflect on how you overcame challenges and the mindset shifts involved.
- Use this journal to reinforce a positive narrative about your abilities.

3. Visualization Techniques:
   - Envision your desired outcomes and successes.
   - Visualize the steps you'll take to achieve your goals.
   - Incorporate sensory details to make the mental imagery vivid and compelling.

4. Affirmations:
   - Create positive affirmations related to your goals.
   - Repeat these affirmations regularly to reinforce a positive mindset.
   - Focus on affirmations that challenge limiting beliefs and foster confidence.

5. Learning from Setbacks:
   - Reflect on past challenges and setbacks.
   - Identify lessons learned and areas for growth.
   - Develop strategies to navigate similar situations in the future with a more positive mindset.

Remember, winning the battle of the mind involves consistent effort and self-awareness. Embrace the process of cultivating a resilient and positive mindset over time.

CHAPTER 4

Safeguarding Your Mind:
The Power of Protecting Your Heart

"So above all, guard the affections of your heart, for they affect all that you are. Pay attention to the welfare of your innermost being, for from there flows the wellspring of life"
- Proverbs 4:23(TPT)

The Fortress of Diligence - A Biblical Tale

In the ancient land of Judah, there lived a young woman named Hannah. She was known for her wisdom, kindness, and unwavering faith in the Almighty. In the midst of a tumultuous era, where the people of Judah faced constant threats and temptations, Hannah's steadfast devotion to God stood as a shining beacon of hope.

One day, as Hannah sat under the shade of an old olive tree, a group of travellers passing by stopped to seek her counsel. They were troubled by the challenges of their journey, the allure of worldly desires, and the fear of losing sight of their faith.

Hannah welcomed them warmly, and shared from the Book of Proverbs:

"Above all else, guard your heart, for everything you do flows from it." (Proverbs 4:23).

She told them of a wise king named Solomon, who had penned those words under the guidance of divine wisdom. She recounted how King Solomon's reign had been marked by prosperity and wisdom, but he had also faced numerous trials that threatened to compromise his heart's devotion to God.

In his youth, Solomon was granted great wisdom by the Lord, but as he grew older, he faced the allure of power, wealth, and worldly pleasures. He was surrounded by foreign influences, and faced the temptation to stray from the path of righteousness.

"As Solomon grew old, his wives turned his heart after other gods, and his heart was not fully devoted to the Lord his God, as the heart of David his father had been." (1 Kings 11:4).

Recognizing the dangers of a heart divided, Solomon urged himself and his people to guard their hearts diligently. He understood that the heart was the wellspring of life, and that from it all actions and decisions flowed. To preserve their faith and stay aligned with God's will, people needed to protect their hearts from the deceptive allure of the world.

"Now all has been heard; here is the conclusion of the matter: Fear God and keep his commandments, for this is the duty of all mankind." (Ecclesiastes 12:13).

As Hannah shared this Biblical wisdom, she emphasised the importance of prayer, seeking God's guidance, and immersing oneself in the Scriptures to fortify the heart against worldly temptations.

She also reminded them of the words of the psalmist, King David, who had also faced his share of trials and tribulations:

"I have hidden your word in my heart that I might not sin against you." (Psalm 119:11).

Hannah encouraged her listeners to follow in the footsteps of these Biblical figures, holding fast to God's Word and diligently guarding their hearts against all that could lead them astray.

The travellers were deeply moved by the wisdom and teachings of Hannah. They thanked her for her guidance and set forth on their journey, carrying the message of guarding their hearts with all diligence as they faced the challenges of their time.

And so the tale of Hannah and the Biblical wisdom of guarding the heart with all diligence became a timeless reminder for generations to come. In the face of trials, temptations, and uncertainties, the steadfast devotion to God's Word remained the fortress that protected the hearts of His faithful followers, guiding them towards a life of purpose, righteousness, and eternal hope.

In the journey of life, our hearts are the core of our being. They hold our emotions, thoughts, and desires, shaping our actions and decisions. Guarding our hearts with all diligence is a vital aspect of living a fulfilling and purposeful life. This chapter explores the significance of protecting our hearts, the challenges we face, and practical strategies to cultivate a fortified heart.

Understanding the Heart

The heart, in this context, refers to the innermost part of our being, the seat of our emotions, beliefs, and intentions. It is the source from which all aspects of life flow (Proverbs 4:23). A well-guarded heart is essential for maintaining mental and emotional well-being, fostering healthy relationships, and achieving personal growth.

Challenges to Guarding the Heart:

1. External Influences:

In a fast-paced, interconnected world, we are constantly bombarded with information and stimuli from various sources. Social media, news, and entertainment can significantly impact our hearts, sometimes leading to negative emotions or harmful behaviour.

2. Past Wounds:

Previous experiences of hurt, betrayal, or disappointment can leave scars on our hearts, making it challenging to trust and open up to others.

3. Negative Thought Patterns:

Negative thoughts and self-doubt can erode the resilience of our hearts and lead to self-destructive behaviour.

Consequences of an Unguarded Heart:

An unguarded heart can lead to various negative outcomes, including:

1. Emotional Instability

Without proper protection, our emotions can be easily swayed, resulting in constant mood fluctuations and difficulty handling stress.

2. Broken Relationships

Unchecked negative emotions can harm our relationships, causing misunderstandings and conflicts.

3. Poor Decision-Making

When we fail to guard our hearts, we may make impulsive decisions driven by emotions rather than rational thinking.

Strategies for Guarding the Heart:

1. Self-Awareness

Developing self-awareness is crucial for guarding the heart. Regularly examine your emotions, thoughts, and triggers to identify areas that need protection.

2. Positive Input
Be mindful of the information you consume and the company you keep. Surround yourself with positive influences, uplifting content, and supportive relationships.

3. Gratitude and Positivity
Cultivate an attitude of gratitude and practise positive thinking. Focus on the good in your life to counteract negativity.

4. Emotional Regulation
Learn healthy ways to manage emotions. Engage in activities like exercise, meditation, or journalling to release negative energy and maintain emotional balance.

5. Forgiveness
Let go of past hurts through forgiveness. Holding on to grudges only poisons your heart and impedes personal growth.

6. Boundaries
Set healthy boundaries to protect your heart from toxic relationships and situations that drain your emotional energy.

7. Seek Wisdom
Surround yourself with mentors, counsellors, or trusted friends who can offer wise advice and guidance.

Guarding your heart with all diligence is a powerful tool for living a purposeful and fulfilling life. By recognizing the significance of protecting our hearts, understanding the challenges we face, and implementing practical strategies, we can cultivate a resilient and fortified heart.

Remember, the journey of guarding your heart is ongoing, requiring commitment and self-compassion. Embrace the process, and your heart will lead you towards a life of greater joy, peace, and fulfilment.

Aphorisms about the Heart:

1. "The heart is the centre of our being, the very essence and core of who we are. It is essential to guard it diligently."
- Emmanuel Jones

2. "In a world of constant distractions, it is vital that you protect your heart from negativity and harmful influences."
- Emmanuel Jones

3. "Your heart is the wellspring of your emotions, thoughts, and actions. Guard it with care and intention."
- Unknown

4. "A guarded heart is a resilient heart, capable of facing life's issues and challenges with strength and grace."
- Emmanuel Jones

5. "In guarding your heart, you preserve the purity of your soul and protect it from the stains of the world and everything therein."
-Emmanuel Jones

6. "When you are standing on Jesus-the sure foundation and corner stone, you will walk through the changing tides of life, your heart will remain steadfast, anchored in truth and love."
- Emmanuel Jones

7. *"Guard your heart against unforgiveness, bitterness and resentment, for they are thieves of joy and peace."* Emmanuel Jones

"Let love be the guardian of your heart, and it will guide you towards compassion and understanding."
- Unknown

8. *"To guard your heart is to cultivate a sanctuary of peace and harmony within your being."*
- Unknown

9. *"The heart is a precious gift; guard it with all diligence and use it to spread love and kindness to all you encounter."*
 - Emmanuel Jones

10. *"In a world of constant change, let your heart be rooted in faith, hope, and unwavering trust in God's plan and purpose."*
 - Emmanuel Jones

REINVENTION TIP 4:
REFLECTIVE EXERCISES:

1. Reflect on your emotional boundaries: Take a moment to consider your emotional boundaries and how well you enforce them. Reflect on situations or relationships where you may have allowed others to cross your boundaries, leading to emotional distress. Consider what steps you can take to establish and maintain healthy emotional boundaries moving forward.

2. Identify toxic influences: Reflect on the people, environments, or habits in your life that have a negative impact on your mental and emotional well-being. Consider the specific ways in which they affect you and whether they align with your values and goals.

Contemplate strategies to distance yourself from these toxic influences or minimize their impact on your life.

3. Practice self-care: Reflect on your current self-care routine and how well you prioritize your own well-being. Consider the activities, practices, or habits that bring you joy, relaxation, and rejuvenation. Evaluate whether you are dedicating enough time and energy to self-care and brainstorm ways to incorporate more self-nurturing activities into your daily life.

4. Reflect on your inner dialogue: Pay attention to the way you speak to yourself internally. Reflect on whether your self-talk is compassionate, supportive, and empowering or if it tends to be self-critical and negative. Notice any patterns or recurring thoughts that undermine your self-worth or confidence. Challenge and reframe these thoughts to foster a more positive and nurturing inner dialogue.

5. Protect your energy: Reflect on the activities, people, or situations that drain your energy and leave you feeling depleted. Consider how you can protect your energy by setting boundaries, saying no when necessary, and prioritizing activities that energize and uplift you. Reflect on the positive impact this can have on your overall well-being.

6. Cultivate positive relationships: Reflect on the quality of your relationships and the impact they have on your mental and emotional health. Consider the people who uplift, support, and inspire you versus those who drain your energy or bring negativity into your life. Reflect on

ways to nurture and cultivate positive relationships while creating distance from toxic or unhealthy ones.

7. Practice mindfulness: Take a moment each day to practice mindfulness and bring awareness to the present moment. Reflect on the sensations, thoughts, and emotions you experience without judgment. Cultivate a sense of gratitude for the present moment and the opportunity to protect your mind and heart from unnecessary stress and negativity.

CHAPTER 5

Unleashing the Power of Your Mind

"Nothing limits achievement like small thinking; nothing expands possibilities like unleashed thinking."
-Williams Arthur Ward

The human mind, an intricate web of thoughts, emotions and perceptions, holds remarkable potential that often remains untapped. This chapter delves into the awe-inspiring power of the mind, exploring the ways in which it shapes our reality, influences our actions, and can be harnessed to achieve extraordinary feats.

Understanding the Mind's Influence
The mind is not confined within the boundaries of the brain; it extends into shaping our experiences, relationships and even physical well-being. Our thoughts create patterns that affect our emotions, behaviour and decisions. This interplay between thoughts and emotions underscores the profound impact of the mind on our lives.

The Power of Belief
Beliefs, whether conscious or subconscious, serve as the driving force behind our actions. If we believe in our abilities, we are more likely to take risks and strive for greatness. Conversely, limiting beliefs can hinder progress and self-realisation. Recognizing and reshaping these beliefs is a pivotal step in unlocking the full potential of our minds.

Visualisation and Manifestation
Visualisation is a tool that bridges the gap between imagination

and reality. When we vividly imagine our goals, we stimulate the same neural pathways that we would if we were actually performing those actions. Mental rehearsal primes our minds for success, boosting confidence and motivation. The concept of manifestation, rooted in focusing our thoughts on what we desire, taps into the mind's capacity to attract and create circumstances that align with our aspirations.

Neuroplasticity: Adapting and Evolving
The brain's incredible ability to reorganise and rewire itself, known as neuroplasticity, underscores the mind's adaptability. Throughout life, our brain's structure and function can change in response to experiences, learning and even intentional mental exercises. This means that we can actively shape our minds through deliberate practice, leading to enhanced cognitive abilities and personal growth.

The Power of Resilience
The mind's power extends to its resilience in the face of challenges. Resilience is not about avoiding difficulties, but about harnessing the mind's ability to bounce back and learn from adversity. By cultivating a resilient mindset, individuals can navigate setbacks with grace and use them as stepping stones toward greater achievements.

Mind over Body
The connection between the mind and the body is undeniable. The placebo effect, for instance, showcases how a belief or expectation can influence physical healing. Moreover, the mind plays a critical role in stress management, immunity and overall health. Techniques such as mindfulness meditation have demonstrated the mind's capacity to regulate bodily functions, emphasising the importance of a harmonious mind-body relationship.

Transcending Limits
Throughout history, individuals have defied conventional

wisdom and shattered expectations by harnessing the power of their minds. Athletes have broken records, inventors have revolutionised industries, and artists have created masterpieces - all through unwavering belief in their abilities and the willingness to push through perceived limits. These stories of human achievement underscore the limitless potential of the mind.

Cultivating Mind Power

The power of the mind is not innate: it is a skill that can be cultivated. Techniques like mindfulness, meditation, positive affirmations and cognitive exercises empower us to harness and direct our mental energy. Just as a muscle grows stronger with exercise, the mind becomes sharper and more resilient with intentional practice.

The power of the mind is a force that shapes our reality, influences our experiences, and propels us toward our goals. It is an instrument of transformation, a catalyst for growth, and a wellspring of potential waiting to be unleashed. As we delve deeper into understanding and harnessing the power of our minds, we unlock the key to creating a life of purpose, achievement, and fulfilment.

Setting the Stage for Mental Unleashing

Before embarking on a journey to unleash your mental power, it is essential to set the stage for success. This chapter focuses on the foundational elements that create the optimal environment for your mind to flourish. By cultivating the right mindset, eliminating distractions, and embracing change, you pave the way for a transformative experience of mental empowerment.

The Power of Intention

Clarifying your intentions is the first step in setting the stage for mental unleashing. What do you hope to achieve through this process? Are you seeking personal growth, professional success, or enhanced well-being? Identifying your goals provides a clear direction and fuels your motivation to embark on this journey.

Embracing a Growth Mindset
Cultivating a growth mindset is paramount to unlocking your mental potential. A growth mindset acknowledges that abilities and intelligence can be developed through effort, learning and perseverance.

By believing in your capacity to improve and viewing challenges as opportunities for growth, you set a positive foundation for mental expansion.

Creating Space for Reflection
In a world filled with constant stimuli, finding moments for reflection and introspection can be challenging. Carving out dedicated time to ponder your thoughts, aspirations and experiences allows you to gain insights into your inner workings. Whether through journalling, meditation or simple contemplation, reflection fosters self-awareness - an essential aspect of unleashing mental power.

Decluttering the Mental Landscape
Just as physical clutter can hinder productivity, mental clutter can obscure your mental clarity. Tackling unresolved emotions, letting go of negative thought patterns, and practising mindfulness help you declutter your mind. This process creates space for new ideas, innovative thinking, and enhanced focus.

Embracing Change and Uncertainty
Change is a constant in life, and embracing it is crucial for mental growth. By stepping out of your comfort zone and embracing uncertainty, you train your mind to adapt, learn and thrive in new situations. Embracing change also involves letting go of attachments to outcomes, which can free your mind to explore new possibilities.

Setting Boundaries

Protecting your mental space involves setting boundaries. This can mean saying no to commitments that drain your energy, or creating technology-free zones to disconnect from digital distractions. Establishing these boundaries cultivates an environment that respects your mental well-being and focuses your energy on what truly matters.

Building a Supportive Network

Surrounding yourself with individuals who uplift, inspire and challenge you is instrumental in mental unleashing. Seek out mentors, friends and colleagues who encourage your growth, provide constructive feedback, and share their experiences. A supportive network creates an ecosystem of accountability and encouragement that fuels your journey.

Cultivating Patience and Persistence

Mental unleashing is a process that requires patience and persistence. Recognize that growth takes time, and that setbacks are part of the journey. Cultivating patience prevents frustration and encourages you to stay committed, even in the face of challenges.

Setting the stage for mental unleashing involves preparing the soil in which your mental power will flourish. By establishing clear intentions, embracing growth, fostering self-awareness and creating a conducive environment, you lay the groundwork for an empowering journey of self-discovery and transformation. This chapter marks the beginning of your quest to harness your mental prowess and realise your full potential.

Exploring the Different Facets of Mental Power

The human mind is a multifaceted gem, possessing an array of capabilities that when cultivated can lead to extraordinary achievements. This chapter delves into the diverse dimensions of mental power, highlighting how cognitive abilities, emotional intelligence, creativity and focus collectively contribute to your overall mental prowess.

Cognitive Abilities:

1. Critical Thinking
The ability to analyse, evaluate and synthesise information is the heart of critical thinking.. Developing this skill enables you to make well-informed decisions, solve complex problems, and navigate challenges with greater efficiency.

2. Logical Reasoning
Logic forms the basis of sound decision-making and problem-solving.. Enhancing your logical reasoning skills allows you to identify patterns, deduce conclusions and construct valid arguments.

3. Memory Enhancement
A sharp memory is a cornerstone of mental power. Techniques such as mnemonic devices, visualisation and spaced repetition can be employed to boost your memory and recall abilities.

Emotional Intelligence:

1. Self-Awareness
Understanding your own emotions, triggers and thought patterns is essential for emotional intelligence. Self-awareness enables you to manage your emotions effectively and respond to situations in a balanced manner.

2. Empathy
Empathy involves recognizing and understanding the emotions of others. Cultivating empathy fosters better interpersonal relationships, effective communication and the ability to connect on a deeper level.

3. Emotion Regulation

The capacity to manage your own emotions, especially in challenging situations, is a hallmark of emotional intelligence. By regulating your emotions, you maintain mental clarity and prevent impulsive decision-making.

Creativity and Imagination:

1. Divergent Thinking
This form of thinking encourages generating a wide range of ideas, often straying from conventional paths. Divergent thinking is crucial for innovation, problem-solving and envisioning unique solutions.

2. Mindful Creativity
By integrating mindfulness practices into your creative process, you can tap into the present moment, allowing ideas to flow organically and sparking new perspectives.

3. Combining Ideas
Creativity often involves merging seemingly unrelated concepts. The ability to synthesise diverse ideas leads to the creation of novel and ground-breaking concepts.

Focus and Concentration:

1. Deep Work
Deep work is a state of intense focus where you immerse yourself in a task free from distractions. This level of concentration enhances productivity, quality of work, and the efficiency of learning.

2. Mindfulness in Focus
Incorporating mindfulness into your concentration practices enhances your ability to stay present in the moment, minimising wandering thoughts and boosting attention span.

3. Flow State

The flow state is characterised by complete absorption and immersion in an activity. Achieving a flow state leads to heightened performance, creativity and a sense of timelessness.

Integration and Synergy

While these facets of mental power might appear distinct, they are interconnected and can reinforce one another. For instance, creativity can enhance problem-solving, emotional intelligence supports effective communication, and cognitive abilities contribute to sound decision-making. By recognising the synergies between these facets, you can holistically enhance your mental power.

Exploring the various facets of mental power is a journey of self-discovery and growth. Each dimension - cognitive abilities, emotional intelligence, creativity and focus - adds a unique layer to your mental prowess. By nurturing these facets and understanding their interplay, you unlock the potential to achieve remarkable feats and lead a fulfilling life driven by your enhanced mental capabilities.

Removing Mental Barriers

Unleashing your mental power requires breaking free from the chains of limiting beliefs, negative self-talk, and fear of failure. This chapter delves into the crucial process of identifying and dismantling these mental barriers, enabling you to pave the way for a more empowered and confident mindset.

Identifying Limiting Beliefs

1.Self-Reflection

Begin by introspectively examining your thoughts and beliefs. Are there recurring patterns of self-doubt or negativity?

Identifying these limiting beliefs is the first step towards dismantling them.

2. Root Causes
Understand the origins of your limiting beliefs. Often they stem from past experiences, societal conditioning, or comparisons with others. Recognizing the root causes helps you address them at their source.

Overcoming Fear of Failure:

1. Reframing Failure
Shift your perspective on failure. Instead of viewing it as a dead end, see it as a stepping stone to learning and growth. Embrace failure as an opportunity for improvement.

2. Courageous Action
Taking action despite the fear of failure is crucial. Start with small steps and gradually build your confidence. Each success, no matter how small, reinforces your ability to overcome challenges.

Cultivating a Growth Mindset:

1. Embrace Challenges
A growth mindset thrives on challenges. Instead of avoiding difficulties, welcome them as chances to learn, adapt and evolve.

2. Embrace Effort
Understand that effort is the path to mastery. Embracing the process of improvement rather than seeking instant success aligns with a growth mindset.

Transforming Negative Self-Talk:

1. Awareness
Pay attention to your inner dialogue. Are you overly critical of yourself? Awareness allows you to recognize negative self-talk patterns.

2. Positive Affirmations
Counter negative self-talk with positive affirmations. Replace self-doubt with self-encouragement, gradually rewiring your thought patterns.

Embracing Vulnerability:

1. Strength in Vulnerability
Acknowledge that vulnerability is not a weakness. It is a sign of authenticity and courage, fostering deeper connections with others.

2. Stepping Outside Comfort Zones
Growth occurs when you venture beyond what feels comfortable. Embrace discomfort as a catalyst for personal development.

Creating a Supportive Environment:

1. Surrounding Yourself
Seek out individuals who uplift and encourage you. Surrounding yourself with positive influences helps reinforce your efforts to overcome mental barriers.

2. Setting Boundaries

Limit exposure to negativity, whether through media, relationships or environments. Protecting your mental space is essential for breaking free from mental limitations.

Removing mental barriers is a transformative journey that empowers you to harness your mental power fully. By identifying and challenging limiting beliefs, embracing vulnerability, and cultivating a growth mindset, you pave the way for self-discovery, resilience and achievement. The process of dismantling mental barriers is a testament to your strength and determination, ultimately leading to a more liberated and empowered version of yourself.

REINVENTION TIP 5:
REFLECTIVE EXERCISES TO HELP YOU UNLEASH THE POWER OF YOUR MIND:

1. Goal Setting: Take some time to define your short-term and long-term goals. Write them down and break them into smaller, actionable steps. This exercise helps clarify your vision and gives you a roadmap for success.

2. Positive Self-Talk: Pay attention to your inner dialogue and replace negative thoughts with positive affirmations. Remind yourself of your strengths, capabilities, and past achievements. This exercise can boost self-confidence and cultivate a positive mindset.

3. Mindfulness Meditation: Set aside a few minutes each day to practice mindfulness meditation. Focus on your breath, sensations, or a specific object. This exercise helps calm the mind, reduce stress, and improve focus.

4. Journaling: Write down your thoughts, feelings, and experiences in a journal. Use it as a tool for self-reflection, gratitude, and problem-solving. This exercise can enhance self-awareness and provide clarity.

5. Visualization: Imagine yourself accomplishing your goals or overcoming challenges. Visualize the details, emotions, and outcomes. This exercise helps build motivation and trains your mind to focus on success.

CHAPTER 6
"Thoughts" - The Blueprint of Your Life.

"The quality of your thoughts determines the blueprint of your life. Your thoughts are the blueprint that shapes your reality and guides you towards your dreams and goals" Emmanuel Jones

THE BLUEPRINT ANALOGY
Unveiling the Blueprint Concept

In this chapter, we will explore the intriguing analogy between thoughts and a blueprint. Just like a blueprint serves as a guide for constructing a building, our thoughts act as a blueprint for shaping our lives. By understanding this concept, we can gain valuable insights into the power and significance of our thoughts.

1. Drawing parallels between thoughts and a blueprint:
Our thoughts are not merely fleeting ideas or random musings. They are the building blocks of our reality. Just as a blueprint provides a detailed plan for a construction project, our thoughts provide the framework for our lives. Just like an architect carefully designs and maps out every aspect of a building, we have the ability to shape our lives through the thoughts we choose to entertain.

Moreover, just as a blueprint captures the vision and intention of the architect, our thoughts reflect our desires, beliefs, and aspirations. They hold the potential to create a life that aligns with our deepest values and dreams.

2. Understanding how thoughts lay the foundation for life:
Every action, decision, and outcome in our lives can be traced back to our thoughts. Our thoughts shape our beliefs, which in turn influence our attitudes, actions, and ultimately, our outcomes. Just as a blueprint provides the foundation upon which a building is constructed, our thoughts lay the groundwork for the life we experience.

When we have positive and empowering thoughts, we create a solid foundation for success and happiness. Conversely, negative and limiting thoughts can lead to self-sabotage and a life that falls short of our potential. By recognizing the power of our thoughts and actively choosing thoughts that support our growth and well-being, we can build a fulfilling and purposeful life.

Designing Your Blueprint:

> A. Taking a Conscious Approach to Shaping Thoughts

1. The Power of Awareness:

In the intricate process of designing your life's blueprint, the first step is cultivating a heightened awareness of your thoughts. By consciously observing the patterns and quality of your thoughts, you gain insight into the foundation upon which your experiences are built. This section explores the transformative impact of mindfulness, encouraging you to be present in the moment and discern the thoughts that contribute to or hinder your growth.

2. Filtering the Negative, Embracing the Positive:

Delving into intentional thought-shaping requires the conscious filtration of negativity. Learn to identify and challenge self-limiting beliefs, replacing them with positive affirmations that align with your goals and aspirations. This part of the chapter equips you with tools to break free from destructive thought patterns, fostering a mindset conducive to success, joy, and personal fulfilment.

Implementing Strategies for Intentional Thought Development:

1. Crafting Positive Affirmations:

Affirmations are the building blocks of your mental blueprint. Uncover the art of crafting positive and impactful affirmations tailored to your unique journey. This section provides guidance on selecting words that resonate deeply, empowering you to instill confidence, resilience, and optimism into the very fabric of your thoughts.

2. Visualization Techniques:

Implementing intentional thought development involves harnessing the power of visualization. Explore techniques that allow you to vividly imagine your desired outcomes, fostering a sense of belief and expectancy. This part of the chapter demonstrates how visualization aligns your thoughts with your goals, reinforcing the blueprint for the life you aspire to live.

3. Establishing Thought Rituals:

Consistency is key in shaping thoughts intentionally. Discover the effectiveness of thought rituals – daily practices designed to anchor positive thinking into your routine. Whether through journaling, meditation, or gratitude exercises, establish rituals that contribute to the steady construction of a resilient and purposeful mental blueprint.

As you delve into the strategies outlined in this chapter, remember that designing your blueprint is an ongoing, conscious process. With each intentional thought, you lay another brick in the foundation of the life you are actively creating.

Explore practical strategies for harnessing the power of thoughts to create the life you desire.

A. The Canvas of Emotions:

In the intricate tapestry of your life, emotions are the vibrant threads that weave the most captivating patterns. They are the colours that paint the canvas of your existence. Just like an artist carefully selects their palette, you too have the power to choose the emotions that define your masterpiece. Emotions are not just spontaneous reactions to external events: they are the result of your thoughts and perceptions, and they can shape the very blueprint of your life.

B. The Emotion-Reality Connection

Imagine for a moment that your mind is a stage, and your emotions are the actors performing on it. The thoughts you entertain are the scripts, and your emotions bring those scripts to life. This is a fundamental principle; your emotions are a reflection of your thoughts. It is not the events themselves that determine how you feel, but rather your interpretation of those events.

Let's take an example. Imagine you receive a rejection letter from a job you applied for. Your immediate reaction might be sadness or frustration. But remember, the event itself is neutral: it is your interpretation of the rejection that triggers these emotions. If you view the rejection as a failure, you will feel downcast. However, if you perceive it as an opportunity for growth and a chance to find a better fit, you will feel hopeful and motivated.

C. Mastering Emotional Intelligence

Understanding the connection between thoughts and emotions is the first step in mastering your emotional intelligence. Emotional intelligence is the ability to recognize, understand, manage and influence your own emotions and the emotions of others. It is a crucial skill for creating the life you desire.

To harness the power of emotions, start by becoming an observer of your thoughts. Pay close attention to the internal dialogue that plays out in your mind. Are your thoughts predominantly positive, negative, or somewhere in between? Are you often ruminating on past mistakes or worrying about the future? The thoughts you consistently entertain have a profound impact on your emotional state.

D. Reframing Your Thoughts

Once you have identified your thought patterns, you can begin to reframe them. This is like rewriting the script for the emotional actors on your mental stage. Instead of dwelling on what went wrong, focus on what you can learn from the experience. Replace self-criticism with self-compassion. Instead of fixating on what might go wrong in the future, concentrate on the steps you can take to create a brighter tomorrow.

Remember, you have the power to choose your emotional palette. You can paint your canvas with a broad spectrum of emotions, each contributing to the richness of your life. By mastering your emotions, you can turn setbacks into opportunities, challenges into stepping stones, and pain into growth.

E. Emotions as Guidance

Emotions are not just tools for internal transformation; they also serve as valuable guides in the external world. They provide insights into your values, desires and boundaries.

When you feel joy, it is often a sign that you are aligned with your values and passions. When you feel anger, it may signal that a boundary has been crossed. When you feel sadness, it could be an indication that something in your life needs attention or healing.

Embrace your emotions as messengers, not as obstacles. They offer clues about the direction your life should take. When you listen to them with curiosity and compassion, you can make choices that align with your authentic self.

Your life's blueprint is an intricate design shaped by your thoughts and emotions. Understanding the connection between the two and mastering your emotional intelligence empowers you to craft a life filled with purpose, joy and fulfilment. Embrace your emotions as the vibrant colours of your canvas, and remember that you hold the brush that paints your unique masterpiece.

In conclusion, understanding thoughts as the blueprint of life emphasizes the transformative power of intentional thinking. By cultivating awareness, filtering negativity, and embracing positive thoughts, you become the architect of your destiny. Crafting affirmations, employing visualization, and establishing thought rituals are tools that shape an evolving masterpiece. Your life's blueprint is not static but a dynamic canvas influenced by your intentional thoughts. With purpose, positivity, and continuous effort, you paint the portrait of your journey, creating a foundation for the masterpiece you will live tomorrow.

Your journey of intentional thought has just begun.

REFLECTIVE EXERCISES:

1. Journal Prompt: Take a few minutes each day to jot down your predominant thoughts. Reflect on how these thoughts shape your emotions and actions.

2. Mindfulness Meditation: Practice mindfulness to observe your thoughts without judgment. Notice patterns and consider how these thought patterns contribute to your daily experiences.

3. Positive Affirmations: Incorporate positive affirmations into your daily routine. Reflect on how these affirmations influence your mindset and overall outlook on life.

4. Identifying Limiting Beliefs: Identify any recurring negative thoughts or limiting beliefs. Reflect on how these thoughts might be holding you back and explore ways to reframe them.

5. Vision Board Creation: Create a vision board that represents your aspirations. Reflect on how your thoughts align with the images and goals depicted on the board.

6. Gratitude Practice: Regularly express gratitude for positive aspects of your life. Reflect on how focusing on

gratitude impacts your overall thought patterns and perspective.

7. Thought vs. Reality: Analyze situations where your thoughts may not align with reality. Reflect on how accurate your thoughts are and if there are opportunities for more realistic perspectives.

8. Setting Intentions: Before significant events or activities, set positive intentions. Reflect on how these intentions influence your mindset and the outcomes of those experiences.

9. Social Media Detox: Take breaks from social media and observe changes in your thought patterns. Reflect on how external influences affect your internal dialogue.

10. Feedback Loop Awareness: Pay attention to feedback from others and reflect on how your thoughts contribute to your interactions. Consider whether adjustments in thinking could enhance your relationships.

CHAPTER 7

Supercharge Your Thinking

- The Joseph Principle

"Each problem has hidden within it an opportunity so powerful that it literally dwarfs the problem. The greatest success stories were created by people who recognized a problem and turned it into an opportunity."
-Joseph Sugarman-

Supercharging your thinking can transform your life drastically. Let us draw inspiration from the Biblical story of Joseph found in the book of Genesis, chapters 37 to 50. In the ancient land of Canaan, this young dreamer faced adversity that demanded a unique mindset. His journey from a favoured son to a slave, and eventually a ruler, exemplifies the transformative power of supercharging one's thinking.

1. Cultivating Visionary Thinking: Joseph's ability to interpret dreams showcased his visionary thinking. Despite the challenges, he held on to the dream of greatness. Supercharging your thinking involves nurturing a vision that transcends current circumstances, much like Joseph did in interpreting dreams of future abundance.

2. Resilience in the Face of Setbacks: Sold into slavery by his own brothers, Joseph could have succumbed to bitterness. Instead, he adapted his thinking, turning adversity into an opportunity to develop resilience. Supercharging your thinking means viewing setbacks as stepping stones, not stumbling blocks.

3. Positive Mindset in Potiphar's House: As a slave in Potiphar's house, Joseph maintained a positive mindset. His dedication and integrity eventually elevated him. Supercharging your thinking involves embracing a positive mindset, even in challenging environments, trusting that your character will lead to breakthroughs.

4. Navigating the Pit and the Prison: From the pit to the prison, Joseph's journey was marked by twists and turns. Supercharging your thinking requires adaptability. Joseph's ability to navigate different situations demonstrates the importance of adjusting one's mindset to the circumstances while holding onto one's values.

5. Interpreting Pharaoh's Dreams: Joseph's moment of significance came when he interpreted Pharaoh's dreams. Supercharging your thinking includes honing your skills and being prepared for the opportune moment. Joseph's expertise positioned him for a role of influence.

6. Forgiveness and Reconciliation: When Joseph's brothers sought help during the famine, he displayed a remarkable mindset of forgiveness and reconciliation. Supercharging your thinking involves releasing grudges and embracing forgiveness, recognizing that this frees the mind to focus on positive growth.

7. Strategic Thinking During Famine: Joseph's strategic thinking during the years of plenty prepared Egypt for the impending famine. Supercharging your thinking involves planning for the future and making wise decisions in times of abundance to navigate challenges effectively.

8. Revelation of Identity: The emotional revelation of Joseph's true identity to his brothers symbolises the profound impact of transformed thinking. Supercharging your thinking leads to self-discovery and the realisation of your unique purpose.

In the saga of Joseph, we find a compelling narrative that

illustrates the power of supercharging one's thinking—a principle applicable to navigating life's complexities with resilience, positivity, and a visionary outlook.

Transforming setbacks into stepping stones or setups:

 Transforming setbacks into stepping stones or setups is a profound journey of resilience and adaptability. Instead of allowing obstacles to be roadblocks, consider them as opportunities for growth and strategic advancement. Embrace the challenges, learn from them, and use the experience as a foundation for reaching higher ground. In the tapestry of life, setbacks can be woven into a narrative of strength, wisdom, and ultimate success. It is not merely about overcoming obstacles, but about leveraging them to propel yourself toward a future filled with newfound possibilities and achievements.

Instead of allowing obstacles to be roadblocks, consider them as opportunities for growth and strategic advancement.

In one of my leadership seminars, I reminded the participants that when life gives one lemons, one should turn them into lemonade.

In the vibrant city of Johannesburg, South Africa, life presented formidable challenges. Jobless and facing an uncertain future, I sought a career change on the encouragement of a friend who suggested greener pastures in Australia. Armed with my accumulated experience, I had enrolled in the Australia Institute of Radiography, in the anticipation of a transformative career shift when I eventually returned to Nigeria.

These hopes were dashed when on the eve of my arrival in South Africa, the reciprocity between the Australian and South African radiography societies was abruptly cancelled. I found myself unemployed, unable to practise radiography, and faced with the need to pivot. Turning to teaching mathematics and sciences in high school became my alternative, yet even that path proved fleeting, as I eventually lost the job.

The turn of the new millennium brought me no joy; unemployment made it a time of struggle just to afford the basics. Depressed and disheartened, I stumbled upon Job 14:7, a verse of scripture that resonated deeply:

"If a tree is cut down, it will sprout again."

I saw myself as that tree, cut down by circumstances, yet this Biblical assurance ignited a spark of hope within me. My mind became supercharged with encouragement from these words.

As the days passed, my faith in a brighter future grew. Eventually, doors opened, and I secured a job in the United Kingdom. I embarked on a new season in my life, leaving behind the shadow of unemployment and embracing a promising horizon.

To those reading this chapter, especially if you find yourself in the midst of difficulties, remember that tough times are transient, but resilient individuals endure. Just as a cut-down tree can sprout again, you too can rise from adversity. Let the encouraging words and verses in this chapter supercharge your thinking, for a brighter future may be just around the corner.

REINVENTION TIP 7:
Here are some reflection exercises to help supercharge your thinking:

1. Question Your Limiting Beliefs: Reflect on any beliefs or assumptions that may be holding you back. Ask yourself if these beliefs are based on facts or if they are simply self-imposed limitations. Challenge these

beliefs and consider alternative perspectives that can expand your thinking.

2. Expand Your Knowledge:
Engage in continuous learning and expose yourself to new ideas, perspectives, and information. Reflect on what you've learned and how it can be applied to your thinking. Consider how expanding your knowledge can open up new possibilities and enhance your problem-solving abilities.

3. Embrace Creativity: Reflect on ways to foster creativity in your thinking. Engage in activities that stimulate your imagination, such as brainstorming, mind mapping, or free writing. Allow yourself to think outside the box and explore unconventional solutions to problems.

4. Practice Critical Thinking: Reflect on your thinking process and evaluate the quality of your reasoning. Ask yourself if you are making logical connections, considering different viewpoints, and weighing evidence objectively. Engage in activities that challenge your critical thinking skills, such as solving puzzles or engaging in debates.

5. Cultivate a Growth Mindset: Reflect on your attitude towards challenges and failures. Embrace a growth mindset, which believes that intelligence and abilities can be developed through effort and learning. Reflect on how adopting a growth mindset can enhance your thinking and lead to greater resilience and success.

Remember, these exercises are designed to enhance your thinking abilities. Feel free to adapt them to your specific interests and goals. Enjoy the process of expanding your thinking and discovering new possibilities!

CHAPTER 8
Transformation by Renewal of the Mind

Renewing the Mind: A Path to Transformation
In this chapter, we will explore the profound concept of transformation through the renewal of the mind. The Bible provides us with guidance and wisdom on how to change our lives by changing our thought patterns and perspectives. As the Apostle Paul wrote in Romans 12:2a,

"Do not conform to the pattern of this World, but be transformed by the renewing of your mind."

The Power of Transformation
Transformation is a process of profound change, a metamorphosis of our character, behaviour and outlook on life. It is not a one-time event, but an ongoing journey. The foundation of this transformation is renewing our minds, which means altering our thought patterns, beliefs and attitudes. By

embracing this renewal, we can experience positive changes in our lives.

Renewal through Scripture
The Bible is a rich source of wisdom and guidance for renewing the mind. Let us explore some key verses that illustrate the power of Scripture in the process of transformation:

Romans 12:2:
"Do not conform to the pattern of this world, but be transformed by the renewing of your mind. Then you will be able to test and approve what God's will is - His good, pleasing and perfect will."

This verse underscores the importance of aligning our thinking with God's will.

2 Corinthians 10:5:
"We demolish arguments and every pretension that sets itself up against the knowledge of God, and we take captive every thought to make it obedient to Christ."

This verse highlights the necessity of filtering our thoughts through a Christ-centred perspective.

Philippians 4:8:
"Finally, brothers and sisters, whatever is true, whatever is noble, whatever is right, whatever is pure, whatever is lovely, whatever is admirable- if anything is excellent or praiseworthy- think about such things."

This verse encourages us to focus on positive, uplifting thoughts.

Practical Steps for Renewal:

1. Daily Scripture Study

Dedicate time each day to reading and meditating on the Bible. It is through God's Word that we gain insight, wisdom and the renewal of our minds.

2. Prayer and Meditation
Spend time in prayer, seeking guidance and transformation. Meditation on Scripture helps us internalise its teachings.

3. Mindful Living
Be conscious of your thought patterns. Recognize negative and destructive thoughts, and consciously replace them with positive, godly ones.

4. Fellowship and Community
Surround yourself with a supportive community of fellow believers who can encourage and hold you accountable in your transformation journey.

5. Mentorship and Coaching

Overcoming Challenges
Transformation through the renewal of the mind is not without challenges. The world bombards us with conflicting messages and distractions. Our own human nature can resist change. However, with faith, perseverance and the guidance of the Holy Spirit, we can overcome these challenges.

Renewing the mind is a lifelong process, but it is the key to true transformation. By aligning our thoughts with God's will and immersing ourselves in Scripture, we can experience a profound change in our lives. As we continue on this transformative journey, remember the words of the Apostle Paul:

"And we all, who with unveiled faces contemplate the Lord's glory, are

being transformed into His image with ever-increasing glory, which comes from the Lord, Who is the Spirit (2 Corinthians 3:18).

Embrace the power of renewal and transformation through the Word of God.

Reflection Exercises on "Transformation by the Renewal of Your Mind"

1. Self-Awareness: Take time to reflect on your current mindset and beliefs. Notice any patterns of negative or limiting thoughts that may be holding you back. Consider how these thoughts are impacting your life and whether they align with the person you want to become.

2. Identify Core Beliefs: Dive deeper into your beliefs about yourself, others, and the world. Reflect on where these beliefs originated and whether they are still serving you. Challenge any negative or self-limiting beliefs and replace them with more empowering and positive ones.

3. Mindfulness Practice: Practice being present in the moment and observe your thoughts without judgment. Notice any thoughts that arise and consciously choose whether to hold onto them or let them go. This exercise helps you detach from negative thought patterns and create space for new perspectives.

4. Positive Affirmations: Create a list of positive affirmations that align with the transformation you want to experience. Repeat these affirmations daily, especially during moments of self-doubt or negative thinking. This

exercise helps rewire your mind with new empowering beliefs.

5. Journaling: Write down your thoughts, feelings, and experiences regularly. Use this practice as a tool for self-reflection and self-discovery. Explore any recurring themes or patterns in your writing and consider how they relate to your mindset. This exercise can help uncover hidden beliefs and facilitate personal growth.

6. Seek Different Perspectives: Engage in conversations with people who have different viewpoints and life experiences. Listen actively and try to understand their perspectives. This exercise expands your understanding and challenges your existing beliefs, allowing for personal transformation.

7. Continuous Learning: Engage in reading, listening to podcasts, or attending workshops that promote personal growth and transformation. Reflect on the new knowledge and insights gained and consider how they can reshape your mindset. Apply what you learn to your daily life and observe the changes it brings.

8. Gratitude Practice: Cultivate an attitude of gratitude by regularly reflecting on the things you are thankful for. This exercise shifts your focus towards the positive aspects of life and helps you develop a more optimistic and transformative mindset.

Remember, the process of transforming your mind requires consistent effort and self-reflection. Be patient with yourself and embrace the journey of personal growth. As you renew your mind, you open yourself up to new possibilities and a more fulfilling life.

CHAPTER 9

Ensuring Sustainable Transformation: Strategies for Long-Lasting Change

The Parable of the Prodigal Son

In Luke 15:11-32, the Scriptures talk about the prodigal son. The story goes thus:

In a distant land, there lived a man with two sons. The younger son, filled with restlessness and longing for a different life, approached his father and asked for his share of the inheritance. Though it was unconventional, the father divided his property between his two sons, and the younger son set off on a journey to a far-off country.

In this distant land, the younger son squandered his inheritance on wild living, living recklessly and without restraint. He found temporary pleasure, but soon found himself impoverished and in despair as a severe famine struck the land. In his lowest moment, he realised the need for transformation.

The prodigal son decided to return to his father, not with the expectation of regaining his position as a son, but merely as a hired servant. He recognized the need for change, repentance, and a new direction in life.

As the prodigal son made his way back home, he rehearsed a confession to his father, acknowledging his mistakes and asking for forgiveness. He was prepared to endure the consequences of his past actions, for he understood that true transformation required humility and accountability.

Upon his return, when he was still a long way off, his father saw him and ran to him. The father embraced his son, showing love and forgiveness beyond measure. He ordered a celebration, saying,

"For this son of mine was dead and is alive again; he was lost and is found." (Luke 15:32).

The parable of the prodigal son illustrates several key principles of ensuring sustainable transformation:

Recognition of the need for change: The prodigal son realised the destructive path he was on, and recognized the need for a transformation.

Repentance and accountability: He confessed his mistakes, and was willing to be accountable for his actions.

Forgiveness and redemption: The father's love and forgiveness played a crucial role in the son's transformation. It emphasised the idea that change is possible, and that transformation can be sustained through grace and mercy.

A new beginning: The prodigal son's return represented a new beginning, an opportunity for lasting change and a transformed life.

This Biblical story serves as a timeless example of how recognizing the need for change, seeking forgiveness, and embracing a new beginning can lead to sustainable transformation and enduring personal growth. It underscores the importance of humility, accountability, and the power of love and forgiveness in the process of change.

The Challenges of Maintaining Long-Term Change
In the preceding chapters of this book, we have explored the remarkable power of reinventing your thinking, and the profound transformation it can bring to your life. We have delved into the intricacies of mindset, the art of positive thinking, and the importance of resilience. Now, as we near the end of our journey together, it is crucial to address a significant aspect of personal transformation: the challenges of sustaining long-term change.

In the journey of personal development and growth, the pursuit of change is only the beginning. The true test lies in the ability to sustain and maintain that change over the long haul. In this chapter, we will explore the strategies and principles that underpin the art of maintaining lasting transformation. It is not enough to make a temporary shift; the goal is to embed change into the fabric of your life, so that it endures and enriches your journey.

The   Cycle   of   Change
Change is not a one-time event, but a cyclical process. Understanding the stages of change can help you navigate the path to lasting transformation. It typically begins with the pre-contemplation stage, where you may not even be aware of the need for change. This is followed by contemplation, preparation, action, and maintenance. The maintenance stage, which we will focus on in this chapter, is where the real challenge begins.

The Pitfalls of Short-Term Thinking   Sustaining transformation is like tending a garden. Just as a garden requires consistent care, nurturing, and protection against weeds, the changes you have made in your life need ongoing attention and commitment. Unfortunately, many individuals fall into the trap of short-term thinking, believing that a burst of motivation or a few weeks of dedicated effort will lead to permanent change. However, this mindset often leads to disappointment when old habits resurface, and progress seems elusive.

The Myth of Overnight Success

In our fast-paced world, we are bombarded with stories of overnight successes and rapid transformations. We see headlines boasting dramatic weight loss, instant wealth, or sudden fame. These stories can create unrealistic expectations, and make us believe that lasting change should happen quickly and effortlessly. The reality of personal transformation is quite different.

The Power of Habits

One of the key challenges in sustaining transformation is the power of habits. Your old thought patterns and behaviours were deeply ingrained, forming habits that became automatic over time. While you have made progress by changing your thinking, those old habits still lurk in the background, ready to resurface when your guard is down.

Strategies for Sustaining Transformation:

1. Consistency: Consistency is the bedrock of sustaining change. Create daily or weekly rituals that reinforce your transformed mindset. Whether it is meditation, journalling, or positive affirmations, make these practices non-negotiable.

2. Accountability Share your transformation journey with a trusted friend, mentor, or coach who can hold you accountable. Having someone to share your challenges and successes with can provide valuable support.

3. Set Milestones Break your long-term goals into smaller, achievable milestones. Celebrate each milestone to maintain motivation and a sense of progress.

4. **Adaptability**
Life is full of unexpected twists and turns. Be prepared to adapt your strategies when faced with challenges or setbacks. Flexibility is a crucial trait in sustaining change.

5.Self-Compassion
Be kind to yourself when you stumble. Remember that setbacks are a natural part of any transformation journey. Instead of dwelling on failures, focus on what you have learned and how you can move forward.

6. **Regular** **Reflection**
Set aside time for regular self-reflection. Evaluate your progress, identify areas where you need further growth, and adjust your plans accordingly.

7. **Surround** **Yourself** **with** **Positivity**
Surround yourself with positive influences, whether it is uplifting books, supportive friends, or inspirational role models. Positivity can fuel your determination.

8. Embracing the Journey
Sustaining transformation is not a destination; it is a lifelong journey. It is about embracing the process of growth, evolution, and continuous improvement. Remember that change is not linear. There will be ups and downs, but your commitment to reinventing your thinking and transforming your life is a testament to your resilience and strength.

Sustaining transformation is a challenge worth undertaking. It is the commitment to living a life aligned with your values, aspirations, and the transformed mindset you've cultivated. By recognizing the challenges and implementing strategies for long-term change, you can continue to experience the profound benefits of reinventing your thinking and transforming your life.

REINVENTION TIP 9:

Reflective Exercises on "Ensuring Sustainable Transformation: Strategies for Long-Lasting Change"

1. Goal Analysis: Reflect on the goals you have set for yourself and your desired transformation. Consider whether these goals are realistic, specific, and aligned with your values. Evaluate whether they are sustainable and will lead to long-lasting change. Adjust your goals if necessary to ensure they are in line with your vision for sustainable transformation.

2. Self-Reflection: Take time to reflect on your current habits, behaviours, and mindset. Identify any patterns or behaviours that may hinder sustainable transformation. Consider what changes you need to make and how you can develop new habits that support lasting change. Reflect on your progress regularly and celebrate small victories along the way.

3. Identify Triggers: Reflect on the triggers or situations that often lead to a relapse or derail your efforts towards sustainable transformation. Identify any negative influences or environments that may hinder your progress. Explore strategies to manage or avoid these triggers and create a supportive environment for your transformation journey.

4. Mindset Shift: Reflect on your mindset and beliefs about change. Consider whether you have a growth mindset that embraces challenges and sees setbacks as opportunities for learning and growth. Challenge any

fixed mindset beliefs that may limit your ability to sustain transformation. Cultivate a positive and resilient mindset that supports long-lasting change.

5. Accountability: Reflect on the importance of accountability in sustaining transformation. Consider whether you have a support system or accountability partner who can provide encouragement, motivation, and guidance along the way. Reflect on ways to hold yourself accountable, such as tracking your progress, setting milestones, or sharing your goals with others.

6. Learn from Setbacks: Reflect on any setbacks or challenges you have faced in your transformation journey. Instead of viewing setbacks as failures, embrace them as opportunities for learning and growth. Reflect on the lessons you have learned from these setbacks and consider how you can apply them to sustain your transformation in the long term.

7. Self-Care and Well-being: Reflect on the importance of self-care and well-being in sustaining transformation. Consider whether you are prioritizing your physical, mental, and emotional well-being. Reflect on activities or practices that nourish and rejuvenate you. Explore ways to integrate self-care into your daily routine to maintain balance and sustain your transformation.

8. Reflect on Progress: Regularly reflect on your progress towards sustainable transformation. Celebrate the milestones you have achieved and acknowledge the positive changes you have made. Reflect on the areas where you still need improvement and develop strategies

to overcome any obstacles. This reflection exercise will help you stay motivated and committed to long-lasting change.

Remember, sustainable transformation is a journey that requires ongoing reflection, adaptation, and commitment. By engaging in these reflection exercises, you can ensure that your transformation is not only meaningful but also enduring. Embrace the process and trust in your ability to create lasting change in your life

CHAPTER 10
Cultivating Success and a Positive Mindset

"The fine, thin line between success and failure is a positive mindset."

- Emmanuel Jones

In the world of personal and professional development, one concept stands out as the bedrock upon which all achievements are built: the Success Mindset. Whether you are striving to excel in your career, improve your relationships, or pursue personal goals, your mindset plays a pivotal role in determining your outcomes. This chapter marks the beginning of an exciting journey into the realms of success, where we will explore the intricacies of developing and nurturing a mindset that not only breeds success, but also empowers you to overcome obstacles and setbacks along the way.

Success is a multifaceted concept. For some, it might mean climbing the corporate ladder and achieving financial abundance. For others, it could be mastering a new skill, nurturing a fulfilling family life, or contributing meaningfully to society. While the specific definitions of success vary, what remains constant is the requirement for a mindset that propels us toward our goals and keeps us moving forward, even when the going gets tough.

Throughout this chapter, we will delve into the core principles that constitute the Success Mindset. We will explore how your beliefs, thoughts and attitudes shape your reality, and how you can harness the power of your mind to steer your life in the direction of your dreams. We will uncover the secrets of successful individuals, from entrepreneurs and artists to athletes and leaders, who have harnessed the potential of their minds to achieve greatness.

8 Mindsets That Will Set You on the Path to Success:

1.Embrace a Growth Mindset According to Joyce Zimmerman, the most crucial step you can take is to adopt a growth mindset. This mindset empowers you to dream big and stretch the boundaries of your ideas to new horizons. Zimmerman endorses the maxim, *"Everything on the way rather than in the way,"* which stems from leading educator Dr. John Demartini.

Instead of categorising experiences as successes or failures, frame them positively. Acknowledge that challenges and obstacles are opportunities for growth and self-improvement.

Another mindset expert, Carol Dweck, highlights that if you are not in a growth mindset, you likely have a fixed mindset, which can hinder your capacity to achieve new milestones.

2. No Risk, No Reward "Sometimes you just have to take a leap of faith," says Zimmerman. Stepping out of your comfort zone and pushing your mental boundaries will make your mind more agile. Consequently, you will learn to reach new heights. Those who shy away from leaving their comfort zone often end up trapped in a fixed mindset. A reluctance to take risks stifles progress and leads to stagnation.

3. Embrace Your Mistakes and Move On Part of taking risks is the ability to learn from your mistakes. A misstep can serve as a valuable lesson, offering you the chance to pivot towards new opportunities. Rather than hiding or making excuses for your mistakes, consider what you can extract from these experiences as you forge ahead.

4.   **Cultivate**   **Curiosity**

No matter your level of education, the quest for knowledge should be a lifelong pursuit, according to Zimmerman. She emphasises that an insatiable curiosity is essential for seeing beyond the immediate and realising your true potential. Continuous curiosity keeps you in a growth mindset, allowing you to explore what lies beyond your current horizons.

5. Find Gratitude and Celebrate Others' Success

Zimmerman stresses the importance of cultivating gratitude by genuinely celebrating the successes of others. Doing so will help you shed feelings of bitterness or resentment, and allow you to focus on your own positive accomplishments. Resenting or being upset about others' achievements can hinder your own success.

6.   **Surround**   **Yourself**   **with**   **Positivity**

As motivational speaker Jim Rohn noted, *"You are the average of the five people you spend the most time with."* Therefore, your mindset will mirror the information you feed it. It is crucial to saturate your mind with positive information daily. Surrounding yourself with positive influences can help you become your best self.

7.   **Prioritise**   **Mental**   **and**   **Physical**   **Health**

Mental and physical agility are both vital components. Zimmerman advocates embracing both, as they complement each other to keep you alert and focused. Maintaining a healthy body and mind generates more positive thoughts than negative ones, and helps you take the daily actions necessary for your priorities.

8   Maintain   High   Energy

When your energy levels are low, and you neglect exercise, negativity can creep in, allowing negative thoughts to take root. Maintaining high energy levels is essential for maintaining momentum, especially in business, where drive and endurance are necessary for managing daily activities.

How a Positive Mindset Can Transform Your Life:

Life is full of setbacks, so why not give up? Because anything is possible with the right mindset.

Have you ever thought, *"My situation has always been the same - I'm stuck, and I must play the hand I've been dealt?"*

Such thinking can drag you down with a fixed mindset. A growth mindset, on the other hand, enables you to thrive despite challenges and obstacles, viewing them as catalysts for growth rather than personal failures.

Failures or setbacks are not indicative of your abilities, but rather opportunities for learning and growth. Embracing a growth mindset means embracing change, learning, and further developing your knowledge and insight.

To Succeed, Turn Your Fixed Mindset into a Growth Mindset

Using failure as a learning opportunity and embracing challenges can be powerful allies on your path to success.

Carol Dweck's research on mindset underscores the profound impact of our mindsets on our level of success. Embracing a growth mindset is the key to your success.

Traits of a Fixed Mindset:

1. The belief that innate abilities are fixed and unchangeable

2. Avoidance of challenges and a fear of failure

3. A focus on judging oneself and feeling threatened by others' success

4. Resistance to criticism and a preference for avoiding challenges

5. The tendency to make excuses when faced with difficulty.

Traits of a Growth Mindset:

1. Eagerness for growth and new experiences

2. Belief in the potential for improvement through effort and learning

3. Inspiration drawn from others' successes

4. Determination in the face of challenges

5. An understanding that setbacks are temporary and opportunities for learning.

"The world is always rich in opportunities, but only for those who can see and seize them." - Unknown

Six Ways to Develop a Growth Mindset:

1. **Continual** **Learning**
Always seek opportunities for learning and growth. Challenge yourself to embrace obstacles and gain new knowledge and skills. Continuous learning fuels personal and professional growth.

2. **Perseverance**
Embrace challenges and obstacles as opportunities for growth, viewing setbacks as temporary situations that can be overcome through determination and resilience.

3.   Embrace   Challenge

Challenges are an integral part of any worthwhile endeavour. Embrace them as opportunities for character development and growth. Confronting challenges builds resilience and humility.

4.   Embrace   Failure

Failure is a matter of perspective. View it as a learning experience that offers valuable insights. Accepting and learning from failure is key to success.

5. Be Open to Feedback

Be open to feedback, as it helps you improve. Effective feedback provides insight into areas of improvement and showcases your progress.

6. Celebrate Others

Celebrate the successes of others genuinely, and avoid jealousy or intimidation. Your ability to genuinely celebrate others' achievements reflects your maturity and self-belief.

By adopting a growth mindset and actively cultivating these mindsets and practices, you can unlock your full potential and set yourself on the path to success.

11 Ways Successful People Think:

This session discusses various ways of thinking that can contribute to success. Here is a summary of each key thinking approach:

1. Big-Picture Thinking

Big-Picture Thinking involves seeing the broader view, understanding what others might miss, and navigating uncharted territory. It helps in scenario planning, which important for anticipating obstacles and defining outcomes. The example of Apple adjusting its health app for the healthcare industry illustrates this concept.

2. Creative Thinking

Creative Thinking is the ability to break free from conventional thinking and explore innovative solutions. It focuses on generating a higher number of quality solutions.

3. Realistic Thinking
Realistic Thinking is about recognizing facts and building certainty. It involves acknowledging the gap between the present and the desired future, avoiding linear thinking, and being patient during growth phases. The example of Campbell Soup Company's transformation in response to its challenges demonstrates this form of thinking.

4. Strategic Thinking
Strategic Thinking is the act of planning for the future by connecting ideas and making early and continuous connections. It comprises five elements: thinking consistently, within context, on the front end, with others in mind, and with a return in mind. The success story of Marvel Studios is used to illustrate this thinking.

5. Possibility Thinking
Possibility Thinking involves seeing solutions in seemingly impossible situations and maintaining a positive life stance. It is a mindset that helps you view opportunities even in the face of failure. The story of chef Jose Andres and his work in Puerto Rico after Hurricane Maria demonstrates this thinking.

6. Reflective Thinking
Reflective Thinking involves evaluating experiences to learn from successes and failures. It entails asking questions about feelings, thoughts and knowledge. The chapter mentions the consequences of neglecting reflection based on research by Daniel Patrick Forrester.

7. Popular Thinking
Popular Thinking is the uncritical acceptance of common

wisdom without questioning assumptions. Uncommon thinking, on the other hand, requires asking questions, challenging norms, and seeking diverse perspectives. The example of "groupthink" leading to poor decisions is provided.

8. Shared Thinking
Shared Thinking emphasises collaborating with others to enhance ideas and solutions. It involves seeking different perspectives, understanding others' experiences, and leveraging expertise. The importance of shared vision and thinking in leadership and decision-making is highlighted.

9. Unselfish Thinking
Unselfish Thinking is about adding value to others and giving back. It involves using your unique skills and resources to help those in need. The story of Robert F. Smith's Morehouse College graduates is a prime example.

10. Bottom-Line Thinking
Bottom-Line Thinking focuses on achieving results and getting a return on investment. It involves aiming to be the best at one thing, building a team around that goal, and delivering value to people. The emphasis is on doing fewer things for greater impact.

11. Focused Thinking
Focused Thinking is characterised by intense concentration to gain clarity and solve specific challenges. Creating a focused environment and reducing distractions are crucial for effective, focused thinking. It leads to better task prioritisation, reduced stress, and enhanced presence of mind.

Each type of thinking has its unique advantages and is essential in different situations. Successful individuals often incorporate a combination of these thinking styles to address various challenges and opportunities.

REINVENTION TIP 10:
Reflection exercises to help you cultivate success and a positive mindset:

1. Gratitude Practice: Reflect on the things you are grateful for in your life. Take a few moments each day to write down three things you are grateful for. Reflect on the positive aspects of your life and the opportunities that have come your way. Cultivating gratitude can shift your mindset towards positivity and attract more success into your life.

2. Celebrate Achievements: Reflect on your past achievements, no matter how big or small. Take time to acknowledge and celebrate your successes. Reflect on the skills, qualities, and efforts that contributed to those achievements. This exercise can boost your confidence and reinforce a positive mindset.

3. Positive Self-Talk: Reflect on your self-talk and inner dialogue. Notice any negative or self-limiting thoughts that may arise. Challenge those thoughts and replace them with positive and empowering affirmations. Reflect on how positive self-talk can shape your mindset and support your journey towards success.

4. Learn from Setbacks: Reflect on any setbacks or failures you have experienced. Instead of dwelling on them, focus on the lessons learned. Ask yourself what you can take away from those experiences and how you can grow from them. Reflect on how setbacks can be opportunities for growth and resilience.

5. Visualize Success: Spend time visualizing your desired success. Imagine yourself achieving your goals and experiencing the positive outcomes. Reflect on the emotions, actions, and mindset of your successful self. Visualization can help align your thoughts and actions with your desired success.

6. Surround Yourself with Positivity: Reflect on the people and environments you surround yourself with. Consider whether they contribute to a positive mindset and support your success. Reflect on any changes you can make to create a more positive and supportive network.

Remember, cultivating success and a positive mindset is an ongoing practice. These reflection exercises can help you shift your perspective, build resilience, and attract more success into your life. Adapt them to your preferences and goals, and enjoy the journey towards a positive and successful mindset!

CHAPTER 11
Embrace Your New Beginning

Now that you have reached the final chapter of this book, I congratulate you on embarking on this remarkable journey of self-discovery and transformation. You have explored the depths of your mind, challenged your existing thought patterns, and discovered the incredible power of reinventing your thinking. It has been a journey of self-realisation, growth, and most importantly, change. But now it is time to bring it all together and set the stage for your new beginning.

The Art of Reinvention

Throughout this book, we have delved into the concept of reinventing your thinking, and you have witnessed first-hand how it can radically transform your life. Reinvention is not about discarding your past or denying your history; it is about using the experiences, knowledge and lessons you have gathered along the way to construct a more empowered and fulfilling future. It is about embracing change as a constant companion on your life's journey.

Think of your mind as a canvas, and your thoughts as the brushstrokes that create your reality. By consciously choosing the colours and patterns, you can paint a beautiful masterpiece that reflects your true desires, values and aspirations. Embrace the art of reinvention as an ongoing, creative process - one that evolves as you do.

The Power of Mindset

One of the key takeaways from this book should be the profound impact of your mindset on your life. You have learned that shifting from a fixed mindset to a growth mindset can unlock your potential and open doors to previously unattainable possibilities. Your thoughts are the architects of your reality, and by adopting a positive, growth-oriented mindset, you lay the foundation for a remarkable life.

Remember that your thoughts are not set in stone: they are malleable and subject to change. When faced with challenges, setbacks, or self-doubt, remind yourself of the principles you have learned in this book. Your mindset can be your greatest ally, helping you overcome obstacles and turn adversity into opportunity.

Cultivating Gratitude

Gratitude is another essential element in your journey of transformation. It is easy to get caught up in the pursuit of bigger goals and brighter futures, but it is equally important to appreciate the present moment and all that you have. By cultivating gratitude, you infuse your life with positivity and appreciation for the simple joys that surround you.

Take a moment each day to reflect on the things that you are grateful for. Whether it is the support of loved ones, the beauty of nature, or the opportunities that have come your way, acknowledging your blessings can enhance your overall well-being and perspective.

Your Roadmap to Transformation

Throughout this book, you have created a personalised roadmap to transformation. You have set goals, established new habits, and practised mindfulness. This roadmap is not a static document, but a living, breathing guide that adapts to your evolving needs and aspirations.

As you move forward on your journey, remember that transformation is not a destination, but a continuous process. Embrace change as a constant companion and view setbacks as stepping stones to growth. Surround yourself with positive influences, seek knowledge, and stay committed to your personal development.

The Ripple Effect

Your journey of reinvention and transformation does not only affect you; it has a ripple effect on the world around you. By becoming the best version of yourself, you inspire and uplift those in your sphere of influence. Your positivity, resilience and growth mindset can be contagious, sparking positive change in others.

Share your story, your struggles and your triumphs with others. Encourage them to embark on their own journeys of transformation. Remember that we are all interconnected, and the positive changes you make in your life can create a ripple effect that touches the lives of many.

REINVENTION TIP 11:

Reflection Exercises:

1. Journaling Your Why: Write about the reasons behind your desire for reinvention. Reflect on how understanding your motivations helps you stay committed to your new beginning.

2. Vision Board for Reinvention: Create a vision board depicting the aspects of your new life. Reflect on how visualizing your goals enhances your commitment to the reinvention process.

3. Letting Go Exercise: Identify aspects of your past that no longer serve your reinvention. Reflect on the importance of letting go and making room for new opportunities.

4. Daily Affirmations: Develop daily affirmations related to your new beginning. Reflect on how these positive statements contribute to reshaping your mindset.

5. Learning from the Past: Reflect on lessons learned from past experiences. Consider how applying these lessons supports your journey toward a successful new beginning.

6. Rebuilding Self-Image: Assess your self-image and identify areas for improvement. Reflect on how enhancing your self-perception aligns with your reinvention goals.

7. Networking for Change: Connect with individuals who have successfully embraced new beginnings. Reflect on the insights gained from their experiences and apply them to your journey.

8. Fear Confrontation: Identify fears associated with your new beginning. Reflect on strategies to confront and overcome these fears, paving the way for a smoother transition.

9. Incremental Changes: Break down your reinvention into smaller, manageable steps. Reflect on how these incremental changes contribute to a sustainable and successful transformation.

10. Celebrate Progress: Acknowledge and celebrate milestones along your reinvention journey. Reflect on how recognizing progress motivates you to continue embracing your new beginning.

Remember, the journey of reinvention is a process. Regular reflection on these exercises can help you navigate challenges and stay focused on creating a positive and fulfilling new chapter in your life.

Final Words from Me to You

I want to remind you that you have the power to reinvent your thinking and transform your life. The journey you have embarked on is a lifelong adventure, filled with opportunities for growth, joy and fulfilment. Embrace it with an open heart and an open mind.

As you turn the last page of this book, remember that your story is still being written. Your life is a canvas waiting for your creative strokes, a puzzle waiting for your pieces to fall into place, and a journey waiting for your footsteps to shape its path.

Embrace your new beginning with courage, curiosity and an unwavering belief in yourself. Trust in the process, and never underestimate the incredible potential that lies within you. Your future is bright, and your possibilities are endless. The only question that remains is: How will you continue to reinvent your thinking and transform your life?

The answer is in your hands.

Thank-you for joining me on this transformative journey. Here's to a future filled with endless possibilities, growth and the fulfilment of your deepest desires.

With gratitude and anticipation,

Emmanuel Jones

REINVENTION AFFIRMATIONS:

1. I am committed to my transformation journey to reinvent myself to become the highest, best version of me that God has created me to be. My life is what I make of it and it is a phenomenal one EVERYDAY.

2. My thoughts create my reality, and I choose to cultivate a mindset that empowers positive transformation in every aspect of my life.

3. I release self-limiting beliefs and welcome a mindset of abundance and possibility, opening the door to unlimited opportunities for growth.

4. Change is the canvas upon which I paint the masterpiece of my life. I embrace it with curiosity and enthusiasm, knowing it leads to profound transformation.

5. I am not defined by my past. Every moment is a chance to rewrite my story, and I am the author of a life filled with purpose, joy, and fulfilment.

6. In the face of uncertainty, I find strength. Challenges are stepping stones to a better version of myself, and I navigate them with grace and resilience.

7. I trust in the process of personal evolution. Each day is a chapter in my journey, and I am committed to growing, learning, and evolving.

8. My thoughts shape my actions, and my actions create my reality. I choose thoughts that align with my goals, propelling me toward the life I desire.

9. I am a constant learner, seeking knowledge and wisdom to fuel my personal growth. Every experience is an opportunity to gain insight and evolve.

10. I welcome change as a natural part of life. As I adapt and transform, I discover new facets of my strength, resilience, and untapped potential.

11. Every challenge is an invitation to reinvent myself. I am not bound by circumstances; instead, I use them as stepping stones to a life of purpose and fulfilment.

12. I embrace change as an opportunity for growth, and I trust in my ability to adapt and thrive through every season of reinvention.

13. I release the past and welcome the possibilities of the present. Every day is a chance for me to recreate and redefine my purpose.

14. My potential for reinvention is limitless. I am a constant work in progress, evolving into the best version of myself with each step I take.

15. I view challenges as catalysts for transformation. As I navigate change, I discover new strengths within myself and unlock untapped potentials.

16. I am the architect of my own reinvention. With resilience and determination, I shape my destiny, creating a life that aligns with my truest aspirations.

References:

Acuff, J. (2013) *Start: Punch Fear in the Face, Escape Average, and Do Work That Matters.* Ramsey Press.

Allen, J. (1902) *As a Man Thinketh.* New York, Thomas J. Crowell Co.

Bandler, R., Fitzpatrick, O. et al (2019) *Thinking On Purpose: A 15 Day Plan to a Smarter Life.* New Thinking Publications, LLC.

Bathla, S. (2021) *Intelligent Thinking: Overcome Thinking Errors, Learn Advanced Techniques to Think Intelligently, Make Smarter Choices, and Become the Best Version of Yourself (Power-Up Your Brain).* Independently Published.

Bible, B. (1611) *The Holy Bible King James Version.*

Brown, B. (2010) *The Gifts of Imperfection: Let go of Who You Think You're Supposed to be and Embrace Who You Are.* Simon and Schuster.

Brown, B. (2012) *Daring Greatly: How the Courage to Be Vulnerable Transforms the Way We Live, Love, Parent, and Lead.* Gotham Books.

Brundtland, G. H. (1987) *Our Common Future World Commission On Environment And Development.*

Burns, D. (1980, 2017) *Feeling Good: The New Mood Therapy.* William Morrow Paperbacks.

Byrne, R. (2008) *The Secret.* Simon and Schuster.

Christenson, L. (1984, 2001) *The Renewed Mind: Becoming the Person God Wants You to Be.* Bethany House.

Collins, A. (2000) Natural Capitalism: the Next Industrial Revolution by Paul Hawken, Amory B Lovins and L Hunter Lovins, 1999. Earthscan, xix+ 396 pp, L18. 99 (hbk). ISBN 1 85383 461 0. *Sustainable Development,*

8(3), 165.

Covey, S. R. (1989, 2020) *The 7 Habits of Highly Effective People*. Simon & Schuster.

Cutler, H. C., & Lama, D. (1998) *The Art of Happiness*. Riverhead.

Duckworth, A. (2016) *Grit: The Power of Passion and Perseverance* (Vol. 234). New York: Scribner.

Dweck, C. S. (2006) *Mindset: The New Psychology of Success*. Random House.

Elrod, H. (2022) *The Miracle Morning: The Not-So-Obvious Secret Guaranteed to Transform Your Life (Before 8 AM)*. Simon and Schuster.

Goleman, D., & Intelligence, E. (1995) *Why it Can Matter More than IQ*. Emotional intelligence.

Hendricksen, W. (1955) *Transforming the Mind*.

Hill, N. (1937, 2009) *Think and Grow Rich*. Capstone.

Kahneman, D. (2011) *Thinking, Fast and Slow*. Macmillan.

Kimmerer, R. (2013) *Braiding Sweetgrass: Indigenous Wisdom, Scientific Knowledge and the Teachings of Plants*. Milkweed Editions.

Klein, N. (2015) *This Changes Everything: Capitalism vs. the Climate*. Simon and Schuster.

Kolbert, E. (2014) *The Sixth Extinction: An Unnatural History*. A&C Black.

Lowell, A. L. (1911) Right Thinking. *The Journal of Education*, *74*(3 (1838), 63-63.

Maxwell, J. C. (2009) *How Successful People Think: Change Your Thinking, Change Your Life*. Hachette UK.

McDonough, W., Braungart, M. (2002, 2010) *Cradle to Cradle: Remaking the Way we Make Things*. North Point Press.

McLaren, K. (2010, 2023) *The Language of Emotions: What Your Feelings are*

Trying to Tell You. Sounds True.

Meyer, J. (1995) *Battlefield of the Mind: Winning the Battle in Your Mind*. Harrison House Inc.

Murphy, J. (1963, 2015) *The Power of Your Subconscious Mind*. Amazing Reads.

Norton, R., & Norton, N. (2013) *The Power of Starting Something Stupid: How to Crush Fear, Make Dreams Happen, and Live Without Regret*. Shadow Mountain.

Peale, N. V. (1990) *The Power of Positive Thinking*. 1952. Greenwich: Fawcett.

Piper, J. (1998) *Renewing Your Mind: A Mindset Book for Spiritual Warfare and Victorious Living*.

Raworth, K. (2017) *Doughnut Economics: Seven Ways to Think like a 21st-Century Economist*. Chelsea Green Publishing.

Ruiz, D. M., & Mills, J. (2011) *The Four Agreements (Illustrated Edition): A Practical Guide to Personal Freedom*. Hay House

Sandford, J. L., Sandford, P. (2007) *Transforming the Inner Man: God's Powerful Principles for Inner Healing and Lasting Life Change*. Charisma Media.

Sincero, J. (2013) *You Are a Badass®: How to Stop Doubting Your Greatness and Start Living an Awesome Life*. Hachette UK.

Tracy, B. (2003) *Change Your Thinking, Change Your Life*. MJF Books.

Treat, C. (1997, 2000) *Renewing the Mind: The Foundation of Your Success*. Harrison House Publishers.

Wattles, W. D. (1910) *The Science of Getting Rich*. Elizabeth Towne Company.

Willard, D. (2002, 2021) *Renovation of the Heart: Putting on the Character of Christ*. NavPress.

Zander, R. S., & Zander, B. (2002) *The Art of Possibility: Transforming Professional and Personal Life*. Penguin.

Zimmerman (2023) *Unleashing your Potential: A Journey to Becoming a Growth Mindset Leader*. Independently Published.

BLURB:
Reinvent Your Thinking, Transform Your Life" offers a comprehensive roadmap for personal growth and transformation. From cultivating a positive mindset and practicing self-compassion to reframing challenges as opportunities for growth, this book provides practical tools and techniques to empower readers to take control of their thoughts and create a life of abundance and fulfilment.

Whether you're seeking to enhance your career, improve your relationships, Leadership, Business or find inner peace, this book serves as a powerful resource to help you unlock your true potential. With its insightful guidance and actionable advice, "Reinvent Your Thinking, Transform Your Life" is a must-read for anyone ready to break free from old patterns, embrace change, and create a life that aligns with their deepest desires.

"As a man thinks in his heart, so is he"!

About the Author

Emmanuel Jones is a dynamic and visionary leader committed to making a positive impact on the world. As the CEO of Jones Foundation, a charity dedicated to offering hope to the hopeless and nurturing future leaders, he embodies a passion for transformative change.

A certified Leadership Consultant with the John Maxwell Team, a global organization focused on leadership and business development, Emmanuel also serves as a speaker, life coach, and Destiny Tour Guide. Adding to his diverse roles, he is the Lead Pastor of Fountain of Grace, Wolverhampton, UK, a Parish of the Redeemed Christian Church of God (RCCG).

In his professional life, Emmanuel brings over 30 years of experience as a Diagnostic Radiographer , having transitioned from the NHS after 20 years of service to an independent healthcare provider.

Emmanuel is happily married to Pastor Alvinah Jones, and their union is blessed with three children. They call Wolverhampton, West Midlands, UK, their home. During his leisure moments, Emmanuel finds joy in reading, playing football.
He is a fan and supporter of Wolverhampton Wanderers (Wolves) Football Club. Additionally, he actively contributes to the community as a member of the Wolverhampton Rotary Club, showcasing his continued dedication to serving humanity.

Printed in Great Britain
by Amazon